Coming to Terms With the Potter

"And we know that in all things God
works for the good of those who love him,
who have been called according to his purpose."
Romans 8:28

Robert Christopher Brown

xulon PRESS

Coming to Terms With the Potter
by Robert Christopher Brown

Printed in the United States of America

Library of Congress Control Number: 2002101197
ISBN 1-591600-23-5

Bible quotations are taken from the New International Version. Copyright © 1978 by New York International Bible Society.

Xulon Press
11350 Random Hills Road
Suite 800
Fairfax, VA 22030
(703) 279-6511
XulonPress.com

To order additional copies, call 1-866-909-BOOK (2665).

Dedication

=====================================

To my donor who gave me back the gift of life. Thank you.

Contents

Dedication..v

Acknowledgements ix

*Foreword xi

Introduction xiii

I.   The Phone Call That Rocked My World 1

II.   A Self-Portrait 3

III. The Impending Storm..11

IV.   Emergency Room Confessions..............................15

V.   Diagnosis Confirmed...21

VI.   God's Sovereignty Behind the Scenes....................31

VII. Round One: A Smooth Beginning...........................37

VIII. Seven Days of Hell 41

IX.   Triumphant Homecoming......................................47

X.   Round Two..53

XI.   Round Three: The End or a Delay? 59

XII. Back in the Saddle Again 63

XIII. The Indian Summer Has Ended............................73

XIV. The Heart of the Storm 81

XV.   Finding a Silver Lining..87

XVI. Preparing for the Road Ahead 91

* Written by my pastor.

XVII.	Submitting to the Potter	95
XVIII.	The First Leg	99
XVIX.	Trial by Fire	105
XX.	Alive, But Not Kicking	113
XXI.	One Step Forward, Two Steps Back	117
XXII.	Joy Comes in the Morning	123
XXIII.	A Christmas Blessing	127
XXIV.	Touched by the Death of a Stranger	131
XXV.	New Year's Day '94	135
XXVI.	Ken	139
XXVII.	Two Steps Forward, One Step Back	141
XXVIII.	Haven't We Been Here Before?	145
XXIX.	What a Difference a Day Makes!	149
XXX.	Home Sweet Home	153
XXXI.	Two-Thirds Full	157
XXXII.	Answering Back to the Potter	159
XXXIII.	The Pain of Dependence	167
XXXIV.	The Big Picture	171
XXXV.	Return to the Land of the Living	175
XXXVI.	By Leaps, Bounds, and a Stumble	179
XXXVII.	A Season of Setbacks	183
XXXVIII.	A Season of Discontent	189
XXXIX.	A Change in Perspective	195
XL.	The Great Reversal	197
XLI.	First Things	201
	Potter's Hand	209
	Appendix	211
	Bibliography	221

Acknowledgements

A project of this magnitude is rarely the work of one man. From the very beginning, friends and family have played a role in the production now before you. My parents, my brother David, and my friends April and Chip were an invaluable help when I wrote the earliest drafts of this book. Their suggestions convinced me that I needed to write with my heart as well as my head. I want to thank my colleagues from the Northern VA Christian Writers Association, as well as Susan Gerding, for their helpful editorial suggestions and advice in finding a publisher willing to take a chance on a first-time author. I want to extend my deepest appreciation to my good friend Christi for all her hard work in editing my final manuscript prior to publication. Her precise mind, warm heart, and honest opinions contributed far more than she'll ever know. I also want to acknowledge my CrossCurrent buddies Brian, Scott, Jon, and Tim for holding my feet to the fire and not allowing me to give up on my dream.

If I were to express my gratitude to everyone whom God has used to bring about his healing work in my life, I'd never stop writing. However, the staff and congregation of Christian Fellowship Church in Ashburn, VA will always deserve a special place in my heart. The same can be said for the nurses, physicians, and support staff of Georgetown University Medical Center who provided top-notch medical care when my life hung in the balance. Finally, I want to shower all praise and honor on my Lord and Savior, Jesus Christ . . . my reason for living, giving, and loving.

Foreword

This is not your typical health, wealth, and property message that says simply, "Have enough faith and you will receive your healing." God is more than a vending machine and Rob does not talk about magic words and easy steps to healing.

Rob Brown's story is a story of real faith that struggles in the midst of a real crisis...the kind of crisis that would cause ANYONE to struggle...this is about life and death...there are no easy answers or quick-fix formulas.

I have had the privilege of being Rob Brown's pastor for twelve years and I have watched him through the good times and the bad times and I know his faith is genuine. He did experience a miracle but not the kind that he would have desired. Sometimes, as Rob shares in this story, the greater miracle is the grace and the strength that God provides to enable us to go through the trials than to be delivered from the trials. This is a story that anyone with a sincere seeking heart can relate to and find the courage to go on!

James Ahlemann

Senior Pastor
Christian Fellowship Church

Introduction

Eleven years ago, an episode of the TV series *Highway to Heaven* introduced me to the world of bone marrow transplantation. The story focused on a discouraged teenage girl whose cancer had become resistant to conventional treatment. Only a Bone Marrow Transplant (BMT) could save her, but her odds of finding a donor were slim. On the verge of giving up on life and her dreams of pursuing a career in Marine Biology, it was up to Jonathan (Michael Landon) and Mark (Victor French) to convince her otherwise. As I watched the drama unfold, I marveled over how agonizing it must be to decide between a slow, painful death or a radical medical procedure that provides no guarantee of long-term survival. A few years later, I found myself in her shoes.

We've come a long way since the first BMT was performed in 1968. Marrow, stem cell, and more recently, umbilical cord blood transplants, are now standard procedures for treating an array of cancers, nonmalignant diseases, and immune system disorders. Included among these are the leukemias, which account for approximately five percent of all cancer cases.[1] Of the multitudes of cancer recovery books that fill the database of Amazon.com,

---

[1] National Cancer Institute, *Research Report: Leukemia, 1987 Edition,* (Washington, D.C.: U.S. Dept. of Health and Human Services, 1987) 5.

precious few have been written by BMT survivors.

Readers be forewarned: TV productions often don't convey the depth of physical and emotional trauma that might accompany a BMT, much less one with an unrelated or mismatched donor. I've taken great pains to provide an accurate retrospective of my journey without getting lost in the medical details.[2] Some of what I write is graphic, so I want to reassure prospective patients and their families that my experience is not normative for all BMT survivors. I was a difficult case; the kind of patient nurses and doctors often refer back to years later when post-BMT complications occur on their watch.

The novelty of my experience aside, anyone with a chronic or life-threatening disease can relate to the trials my family and I have faced. The many hours of drafts, redrafts, editing, and procrastination that went in to this project helped me vent my feelings and process how each victory or setback shaped my life. In retrospect, I'm thankful for the trials chronicled in these pages because they continue to teach me about life and the character of God.

I want to share my testimony about God's love and healing power with as many people as possible. Although the medical establishment can treat illness, God is the ultimate source of healing . . . healing of the soul and spirit, as well as the body. He has prolonged my life for a purpose. Part of that purpose is to share my testimony with others and point them to the author of all life: Jesus Christ.

You may never have faced a life-threatening disease. If that's the case, you're very fortunate. Perhaps you rarely get sick, never go to the doctor, and need a reminder every year to visit the dentist. Before you set this book down, let me give you a reality check: I just described myself nine years ago.

Our health histories vary, but we all experience loss and question the goodness of God at some point in our lives. A romantic relationship goes south. A loyal worker loses his job through no fault of his

---

[2] Writer's note: Aided by the firsthand accounts of family, friends, hospital personnel, and nurses' case notes, I've provided a truthful and accurate account of my battle with leukemia. Due to the passage of time, the chronology of minor events is not exact. The same can be said for dialogue. Although I've adapted the wording and flow of certain conversations to suit my editorial preferences, I haven't compromised the integrity of the message.

own. A mother loses her baby to SIDS. God's ways are mysterious. He doesn't always answer the questions that make us toss and turn at night, but he never fails to offer himself as a refuge when there's nowhere else to turn. If my story inspires hope and an abiding faith in the Great Physician, it has served its purpose.

Robert Christopher Brown
Spring 2002

CHAPTER I

The Phone Call That Rocked My World

Nothing about June 24, 1992 set it apart from any other day in Southern California. Smog blanketed the suburbs, motorists clogged the freeways, and tourists flooded the beaches and strip malls. It epitomized the mundane. As I climbed out of bed, poured myself a cup of coffee, and left for a routine visit to the doctor, I never dreamed that my self-deception would come to an end just hours later.

If someone had asked me that morning to name the last person on earth whom I expected to get cancer, my answer would have been me. From kindergarten through graduate school, I missed less than ten days of school due to illness. My last bout with the flu was at the age of five, and outside of the common cold, a sinus infection, or a rare stomach bug, I just didn't get sick. Cancer? That was a disease reserved for everyone else.

That afternoon, one phone call shattered this illusion forever.

"Hello?" I answered, diverting my attention from an afternoon re-run of *Knight Rider*.

"Rob, this is Marsha, the school nurse," the caller said. "I want you to report to the Emergency Room at Whittier Intercommunity Presbyterian Hospital immediately."

1

Shocked to my core, I asked, "Why? What's wrong?"

"The pathologists who examined your blood results from earlier today informed me that your hemoglobin and red blood cells are way below normal," she replied. "However, I'm most concerned about your platelets, the cells that enable your blood to clot. Rob, the average person's platelet count is at least 200,000. Yours are numbered at 17,000."

"W-What does that mean?" I asked, stammering.

"In your condition, a fall or a blow to your head might cause severe trauma or death," she answered. "Listen, I don't know if this is leukemia or not, but something is wrong. I called the hospital to let them know you're on the way. And Rob . . . prepare to be admitted."

When I heard the word "leukemia," a wave of fear engulfed me. With my hands shaking and my head spinning, I hung up the phone and scurried about for my car keys. Ignoring the voice in my head telling me to remain calm and plan a strategy, I was out the door in a matter of seconds, informing no one of my condition. Amidst all of my frenzy, I forgot to pack an overnight bag.

There must be some kind of mistake. It can't be leukemia. It just can't.

Chapter II

A Self-Portrait

Driving alone to the hospital in my condition was foolish, but the word "leukemia" shouted louder than my common sense. As I pulled away from my house and headed down Biola Avenue, I couldn't shake the feeling that I might have climbed behind the wheel for the last time.

Please, God. Don't let it be leukemia. Let it be something else . . . anything but cancer.

Sound familiar? The belief that we're immune to cancer, divorce or bankruptcy is ingrained in many of us. The possibility of such a monstrosity taking place becomes real only when it hits "close to home," as in the case of a friend, family member, or the kid next door.

Folks . . . I **am** the kid next door. The youngest of two brothers, I was born on November 3, 1967 to Dave and JoAnn Brown and raised in the Virginia suburbs of Washington, D.C. Educated in the public school system from kindergarten through high school, I dreamed of becoming an architect until the 8th grade when I discovered it required a keen knowledge of math and science. As a child of the '70s, my heroes were the Six Million Dollar Man, Luke Skywalker, Evel Knieval, and anyone associated with the Washington Redskins. A rock-and-roll rebel, I was fascinated with KISS, especially because my parents disapproved of them. When I was 10 years old, I used to stand in front of my mirror and practice sticking out my tongue like Gene Simmons.

My dad, who hails from Galion, Ohio, graduated from the University of Kansas in 1957 with a degree in Petroleum Engineering. During his first year out of college, he worked in the oil fields of West Texas before he was called to active duty as an officer with the U.S. Air Force. After a three-year stint in the military, he relocated to the D.C. metropolitan area in 1961 and worked as a Patent Examiner with the Federal Government until his retirement in January '95.

Analytical, practical, and good with his hands, my dad can fix anything. The Classic Type A personality, household projects are more than a compulsion with him. They're his "calling." Prudent with his time and money, he was one of the first of his high school peers to purchase a car, and he's the only person I've ever known who claims he never slept through any of his morning classes in college. He's rarely late for an appointment, and the logic of paying for an oil change at Jiffy Lube when you can do the work yourself escapes him.

Although he's sometimes blunt and prone to voice his opinions too quickly, my dad is one of the most honest and humble men I know. Underneath the tough, utilitarian mind of the engineer lies the soft heart of a man who wouldn't think twice about climbing into an icy bathtub to keep company with his feverish four-year-old son. He gives God the credit for his ability to provide for our family, and he's never taken his grace as anything less than a gift of unmerited favor.

My mom is a native of Beckley, West Virginia. Upon her graduation from high school in 1960, she moved to Arlington, VA to take a job with the U.S. Department of Agriculture. There's no doubt in my mind that she could have been a success in the corporate world, but after she married my dad in 1963, she settled down and became the quintessential stay-at-home mom. Today, some might question her choice, but as for me, few things were more reassuring than her greeting, "So, how was your day?" every afternoon when I came home from school.

Never one to "put on airs," my mom isn't impressed by status, income, or level of education. She can discern hidden motives or virtues in people long before they come to light. My dad may be the standard bearer for the family, but my mom is the one who interprets that standard down to everyday affairs. She's the first person I seek when I need advice, and her counsel often begins with the question, "Well, have you prayed about it?"

Both of my parents were involved in my life as a youngster. My mom served as a Room Mother, a Cub Scout Den Mother, and a Little League Team Mother. My dad helped coach one of my soccer teams, participated in Y-Indian guides (a program of YMCA), and served on the Boy Scout council.

There was a downside to their involvement. At least, that's what I thought at the age of 14. They were strict. A 'C' on my report card meant no TV for the next grading period, and cussing or backtalk usually culminated in an afternoon alone in my bedroom. My peers often joked about the hard line my parents took on matters of discipline, but our residence still seemed to be the neighborhood gathering place. My dad was the first person asked to fix a flat bicycle tire, and many of my friends felt no qualms about asking my mom for advice on problems at school.

My brother David and I were high-maintenance kids. Energetic, impulsive, and strong-willed, we ran circles around our parents. I stopped taking naps at the age of 18 months, David developed an unhealthy fascination with electrical outlets, and we both enjoyed flushing clothes down the toilet. Crystal candy bowls, tea sets, and miscellaneous "knickknacks" just didn't exist in our home. My mom learned from early on that placing objects on the coffee table was an exercise in futility. Keeping us from harming each other was enough of a battle.

Born two years younger, my rivalry with David was my religion until high school. We fought over everything from the rocking chair in the TV room to personal air space in the station wagon. No one pushed my buttons as well as he did, and I'm certain he can say the same about me. Our rivalry cooled as we grew older, but a familiar refrain throughout our childhood was my dad's injunction, "David, quit putting Robby down! Robby, stop goading your brother!"

David was the classic extrovert. Outgoing and friendly, he always took the initiative to get to know the new kid on the block and bring him into his circle of friends. I recall several occasions in which I came home from school and saw him playing in our backyard with a group of kids I'd never met. I once thought he knew everyone at school.

David was a good role model because he knew how to make friends, and he wasn't afraid to take risks. When a new fad like skateboarding or BMX racing swept the nation's youth, David took it upon himself to be the most daring, if not the best. Because he was interested in so many things, he often moved on to something else once he proved himself. A graduate of VA Tech, David is now employed as a Civil Engineer. He and Brenda, his wife of ten years, live in Reston, VA.

I was a good kid, but fiercely independent. I balked at everything from going to bed at 9:00 p.m. on school nights to wearing dress clothes on Sunday morning. At school, I gave my teachers fits over how I mastered subjects like reading, spelling, and social studies, yet demonstrated complete ignorance of class rules and procedures like changing into my sneakers before gym or bringing my milk money to school every morning.

My personal style ranged from good-natured to high-strung. My temper often transformed me into my own worst enemy, but at my best, I charmed the cherries right off the trees. Unlike my brother, I vacillated between the extremes of the class clown and the shy daydreamer, and I envied him for his self-confidence.

My life was filled with the activities of a typical American boy. I played soccer for two seasons, bowled for three seasons, and lingered in the outfield for four seasons of baseball. I enjoyed sports, but I often had just as much fun as a spectator. I could go to the snack bar whenever I wanted, and during David's games, I often hung out with my friends at the creek which ran behind the ball park. In addition to sports, I participated in the Boy Scouts, took piano lessons, and played the drums.

I came into my own as a teenager, and I avoided the pitfalls that ruined the lives of some of my peers. Although I spent half of my junior high years on restriction for slipping grades, shooting off at the mouth, and neglecting my chores, I never played hookey or experimented with drugs. I received one day of in-school suspension for fighting during the 7th grade, but I rarely lost my temper when I didn't get my way.

Raised in a Christian home, I came to faith in Christ at the age of nine. My teen years began on a solid foundation because I knew God loved me and accepted me into his family on the basis of his grace and mercy alone. I had no desire to get involved in the party scene because I had something to live for that many of my friends couldn't appreciate.

In my mid to late teens, Christ became the center of my life. I never pushed him on others, but I lived my faith in the open and people knew where I stood. I participated in the music and drama ministries at church, and some friends and I led a prayer and devotional group at school called "The Gathering." For two years, we met every day between 2nd and 3rd period, and at one point during the spring of my junior year, we averaged 50 students a day.

In addition to church and ministry activities, music was a large part of my life. During high school, I played the drums in the Concert Band, Symphonic Band, and Marching Band. I dropped band during my senior year because of a heavy academic load, but I continued playing drums for the praise band at church on Sunday nights and for a Christian rock band some friends and I put together in the Summer of '85. We only performed a few times, but we had a blast.

My personality hasn't changed much since then. I'm friendly and I enjoy people, but on occasion, I still withdraw to recharge my batteries. I'm more likely to be outgoing when I'm with close friends, and I can keep a room full of people in stitches with my dry sense of humor. In social settings with strangers, I sometimes come across as a loner.

In many ways, I'm the opposite of my dad. I don't adhere to schedules unless the situation demands it, and I have little interest in math, science, computers, video games, or automechanics. A born night owl, I function best in the evening and prefer sleeping in until the late morning. During my years away at a school in the Central Time Zone, my dad and I were on such different schedules that I sometimes went to bed the same time he got up for work.

I can't "fake it" when I'm nervous or displeased. One reason I never got away with mischief in elementary school was because I always looked guilty. If I had been the White House Chief of Staff during the Watergate scandal, President Nixon would have resigned before the '72 election.

I rarely lose my temper, but I'm prone to becoming tense and inpatient during times of stress. I sin the most when modern technology (e.g., computers, copy machines) fails to comply with my desires or I'm caught in rush hour traffic. I can also become so consumed with a project that I "zone out" and ignore everything and everyone. Just ask my parents how many times they have to tell me that dinner is on the stove when I'm chatting on-line with my friends.

Most people describe me as kind, easy-going, non-judgmental, and a good listener. I don't sweat the small stuff or expect people to measure up to standards I don't practice myself. I prefer the role of peacemaker whenever possible, but when the situation demands it, I can speak the truth without shaming the person. Perhaps that's why I'm drawn to the field of counseling.

Ever since I can remember, I've been fascinated with human behavior and I've wanted to help people struggling with emotional problems. By the time I graduated from high school in June '86, I had my heart set on becoming a Christian counselor. I was so sure this was God's will that I majored in both Psychology and Theology at Oral Roberts University (Tulsa, OK).

As a student at ORU, I served two years as a member of the Christian Service Council and one year as a student floor chaplain, both of which gave me an outlet for ministry and a means for developing my gifts of counseling, teaching and discipleship. After much prayer and soul-searching, I decided once and for all to pursue the goal of becoming a Clinical Psychologist.

Many of my friends got engaged before I graduated from ORU, but somehow, I always assumed I'd get married later in life. Although I often felt left out because I didn't have a significant relationship, I was building for the future. Three months before my graduation in May '90, I reached my first milestone when I was accepted into the Rosemead School of Psychology at Biola University (La Mirada, CA). One of only two Christian doctoral programs which enjoyed full accreditation from the American Psychological Association (APA), Rosemead had been my first choice all along. When I set out for California that summer, I fully expected to earn my doctorate in five years, find a wife by the end of the decade, and become the next James Dobson before my hair turned gray.

Now, two years later, it looked as if I might not live to see any of it come to pass. My American dream had just become my worst nightmare.

CHAPTER III

The Impending Storm

4:00 P.M., Wednesday June 24

When I pulled into the hospital parking lot, my adrenalin was sky-high. It took me just 15 minutes to move from the initial shock of Marsha's phone call to out-right bargaining with God. *Please, God . . . let it be something else . . . an infection, or maybe Diabetes or low blood sugar. Listen, I'll change my diet, I'll take Insulin, I'll do anything. Just don't let it be leukemia!*

After I checked in at the ER admissions desk, I filled out a questionnaire and took my seat in the waiting room. Moments later, a nurse escorted me back to the ER and hooked me up to an IV to keep me hydrated. After she took my vital signs, she said, "A doctor will see you as soon as possible. In the meantime, don't hesitate to give me a call if you need anything."

For those who have never been treated in the ER, the words "as soon as possible" are euphemistic for "Relax. It's going to be awhile."

Strange as it may seem, I didn't constitute a crisis. My vital signs were normal, I had no signs of internal bleeding, and unlike victims of stroke or cardiac arrest, I walked into the ER under my own power. I spent the next several hours giving multiple blood samples, having X-rays taken of my heart and lungs, and surveying the clock on the wall every five minutes. I saw no doctor and received no answers about my condition. I tried gleaning information about my diagnosis by listening in on consultations between nurses and other ER personnel, but all I comprehended was a nurse's excitement about the upcoming Genesis concert.

Some time later, I got up from my bed to use the restroom, and I was greeted by a man in a white lab coat.

"Excuse me, Mr. Brown?" he asked.

"Yes?" I answered, as he walked over to me. He was an older man with thick glasses and thinning hair. Based on his appearance, I assumed he was someone important.

I think this guy's the head physician of the ER. Perhaps I'll finally get some answers.

"Have you ever worked with hazardous chemicals?" he asked.

"I don't think so," I replied. "Why do you ask?"

"Continued exposure to toxic chemicals has been associated with low blood levels," he said.

"I did use some wood sealant last summer when I had my own deck cleaning and waterproofing business, and my dad and I recently changed the oil and transmission fluid in my car. Outside of that, I can't think of anything else," I said, shaking my head.

"Okay. I was just wondering," he said and left to attend to the needs of other patients.

Toxic chemicals? I know I probably inhaled the fumes from that wood sealant on occasion, but that couldn't be the cause of this, could it? There's got to be another explanation.

Scared, dazed, and bewildered, I made my way back to my bed. I couldn't make heads or tails as to how a trip to the ER figured into God's plans for me. The past two months had been the culmination of my Master's curriculum at Rosemead. Stress, eating on the run, and fitful nights of sleep had defined my life. The dreaded finals, papers left unwritten until the week they were due, mountains of reading that should have been completed months earlier . . . it overwhelmed me. When I started losing weight, eating less, and taking more naps, I just assumed it was par for the course.

I never would have guessed that I was experiencing the first signs of a deadly illness. The onset of leukemia can be so subtle that it's often discovered during a routine blood test to monitor a preexisting medical condition or rule out the presence of an infection. Most individuals with leukemia blow off its initial symptoms as the flu, fatigue, or in my case, the combination of stress and a lingering sinus infection.

By the time I graduated on Memorial Day weekend, I had lost 10-15 lbs. and felt so worn-out that I needed the entire summer to recuperate. Unfortunately, I couldn't afford that luxury because I had to take Advanced Statistics later that June. The only thing close to a vacation that I looked ahead to was a nine-day visit at my parents' home in Virginia. To get there, I drove across the country alone so I could renew my car registration there and save money on taxes and insurance.

The day I arrived home, my mom took one look at me and exclaimed, "Rob, you've lost weight! You look great!"

Any guy who's experienced the mid-20s spread loves to hear this sort of compliment, even if it's from his mom. "Well, I guess it's because I've been exercising and watching what I eat," I answered, stretching the truth to the limit.

At home, I experienced frequent headaches, chronic sinus congestion, poor appetite, soreness in my legs and knees, and an intermittent "pounding" in my head. My parents chided me about seeing a doctor once I returned to California, but I kept putting it off. By the fourth week of June, I felt so run-down and sluggish that getting out of a chair brought spells of dizziness, lightheadedness, and blurred vision. Climbing a flight of stairs felt like a run around the block.

Tuesday evening, June 23, was the last straw. Believing exercise might make me feel better, I went for a run around the Biola soccer field and almost collapsed halfway into my first lap. I knew then that something was wrong.

When I paid a visit to the university health clinic on the morning of June 24, the intern on-call noticed the disparity between my resting and standing heart rate and suggested that I might have a problem with my heart. As he made preparations for me to see a cardiologist, Marsha, the school nurse, stopped him.

"He looks pale," she said.

"What do you mean?" I asked.

"Have you had any recent viruses that we need to know about?" she asked. "Perhaps that could explain your condition."

"I was just telling the doctor that I had a bad sinus infection this past April," I answered.

"Well, I'm going to draw some blood for a routine count," she said. "Just to make sure, I'll test it for Mononucleosis."

"You can do that here?" I asked.

"Sure, it won't take long," she assured me. "Just take a seat in the waiting room. I'll let you know the results in a few minutes."

While I was chatting with the receptionist, a single young lady whom I'd met at church a few weeks earlier, the nurse and doctor came out to discuss my results.

"You don't have mono, but as I suspected, you're anemic," she said. "You've probably been losing blood for several weeks."

"How can that be?" I asked.

"That's what we're trying to find out," she replied. "Rob, I'm going to send your blood to a lab in Orange County to have it analyzed further. I suggest that you return home and get some rest. I'll call you in three hours."

Three hours later, I found myself flat on my back in the ER. My parents, the people I counted on the most when the chips were down, were 3000 miles away in Virginia.

They have no idea where I am or what I'm doing right now. No one does! All of my friends are still at work, and thanks to my haste in getting here, my landlady probably thinks I just stepped out for groceries. I should have called or told someone before I left.

In my darkest hour, no one rushed to my bedside to pray with me, keep me company, or bring me a soda and a fresh change of clothes. That said, I wasn't alone. The One who promised to never leave or forsake me was there all the time.

God, you're the only one I can turn to right now. I have no idea what's going on or why this is happening, and I need your grace now more than ever. Help me know you're still in control.

CHAPTER IV

Emergency Room Confessions

As I lay there asking God to help me through what might be the worst crisis I've ever faced, I did a lot of soul-searching. I reminisced about my childhood and my family, fully aware that I might die of my condition. I thought about how I had come out to CA two years earlier, full of anticipation over what God had in store for me in the future as a Psychologist, a husband, and a father. Now it looked as if I might not have a future at all.

I had no doubt that God could heal me. As a graduate of ORU, the concept of divine healing had been ingrained in me for years. I never questioned whether or not I should pray for someone who was sick. It was a no-brainer. However, despite the myriad of testimonials I'd heard about his healing power, I often struggled with why God doesn't heal everybody and why he allows some people to die, even when they have the faith that they'll get better. The question that haunted me now was, *Why Me?*

Ever since I'd learned to sit through an entire sermon, I'd heard preachers shout from the pulpit, "God is able!" Well, of course he's able. If he can create the universe by speaking it into existence and turn water into wine without so much as a flick of the wrist, he can do anything he wants. The $50,000 question in my mind had always been, "WILL he do it, and if not, WHY NOT?" No one had ever given me a satisfactory answer.

As the clock on the wall ticked off the hours, a question asked by a man of God thousands of years ago came to mind: "Shall we accept good from God, and not evil?"[1] That man was Job, someone with whom I'd never had much in common. As I thought about Job's experience, it was as if God had bent over and whispered,

Why NOT you? What makes you different from everyone else?

It dawned on me that although God never guaranteed that my life would run smoothly, I'd always assumed that he was obligated to protect me from diseases such as leukemia. I couldn't even remember the last time I thanked him for my good health. It was my "sacred birthright."

When I took a hard look at myself, I couldn't help but notice that it had been awhile since I'd thanked God for anything. Confronted with my callousness and pride, I realized that I'd been guilty of something that had its roots in me long before I left for graduate school: self-centeredness.

When I began my first year at Rosemead, I felt overmatched. As one of the youngest students in my class, I had no prior work, let alone life, experience. Several of my peers were married, had advanced degrees, and were employed in mental health settings prior to their enrollment at Rosemead. I didn't know the first thing about being a psychotherapist. Concerned more with how I measured up to the rest of my peers than whether or not I really helped anyone, I lost sight of my reasons for becoming a counselor.

Instead of resting in the assurance that God had called me to be a counselor, feelings of inadequacy consumed me. Plagued with doubts about my suitability for the profession, I regressed in my faith. My prayer life grew stale, my church attendance became sporadic, and I ceased relying on God for strength. I became more impatient with commuters on the freeway, started using language that hadn't been a part of my vocabulary since grade school, and I no longer enjoyed God's peace in my life. By the time I graduated with my Master's degree in May '92, I was on the verge of physical and emotional burn-out. Worst yet, I harbored serious reservations about my choice of career.

---

[1] Job 2:10a

During my two-year stint in California, my relationship with my parents suffered as well. Although I'd attended college away from home, my life in graduate school was my first taste of freedom. I lived off campus, drove my own car, and answered to no one. I enjoyed my freedom, and I didn't want my parents spoiling it. Finances kept me anchored to reality, and I knew I wouldn't be free until I severed the ties to my dad's checkbook. Arguments often erupted when my parents expressed their concerns about how I spent my time and their money.

Don't get me wrong. Our relationship wasn't a complete disaster. I still talked to them on the phone every once and a while, particularly when I needed prayer or encouragement, and I always looked forward to going home for the holidays. Nevertheless, I usually called them merely out of obligation. When they gave me unsolicited advice, I became defensive and told them to stop meddling in my affairs.

Most parents struggle with letting their kids go, but much of the blame for the problems in our relationship could have been laid at my doorstep. Something needed to happen to cause a reawakening in my life. God had never let me stray away from him without sounding a wake-up call. As I waited in the ER pondering my fate, the call was heard loud and clear.

God, for years, I've turned it all around by saying that I exist to serve your purposes, but living as if you exist to serve mine.

It was true. Even though I loved God, I often neglected my relationship with him and prayed only when I needed something from him. In fact, my motivation for serving him as a counselor was fed as much by my own needs for validation as it was by a passion to touch others with his love. Feeling more humbled than ashamed, I laughed to myself at the absurdity of it all.

Lord, you don't owe me a thing. Everything I have is a gift from your hand. Forgive me for my cavalier attitude toward you and for taking your blessings for granted.

Just then, my thoughts were interrupted by the nurse who had started my IV hours earlier.

"How are you doing, Mr. Brown?" she asked.

"Alright, I guess," I said.

"Don't worry," she said. "We haven't forgotten you. We're just trying to find out why your blood levels are so low."

"Is the doctor ready to see me?" I asked.

"Dr. P. is with another patient right now, but he should be with you shortly," she replied.[2]

That's what I heard before. It's past dinner time, and I haven't eaten in hours. What's taking so long?

I returned to my thoughts about Job and considered the possibility that God had a purpose in allowing me to get sick. I couldn't promise that I would follow Job's example to perfection, but I told God that I wanted to learn whatever he was trying to teach me.

Lord, regardless of the outcome, I want to remain faithful to you. I pray that your purpose will be accomplished in my life.

I knew that if I had leukemia, my best chance for survival was to trust God and have a positive attitude. I couldn't afford to get angry at him or throw in the towel if a diagnosis of cancer were confirmed. My eternal destiny was a settled issue the moment I put my faith in Christ, but I wasn't ready to die just yet. I hadn't come close to fulfilling what I believed was God's call on my life.

God, I know you see the big picture. I just want to thank you for giving me 24 years of good health and allowing me to grow up in a loving family who taught me about you. I haven't been on the best of terms with my parents lately, but you couldn't have placed me in a better home. I just give this whole situation to you, and I believe this is all going to work out in the end.

The moment I released myself to God, something unexplainable happened. To this day, I can't describe it as anything other than an overwhelming sense of God's presence and a calm, peaceful assurance that I was going to be alright. God was going to heal me.

I'm not going to die! For some reason, I just know that God isn't through with me and that it's not my time to go. I'm going to beat this thing!

People often ask me how I just "knew" that God was going to heal me. The most common question I'm asked is, "How do you know it wasn't just your survival instincts—a response to the shock

---

[2] Out of respect for the privacy of the physicians in charge of my care, I refer to them by their last name initial throughout my writing.

of hearing you might have cancer?"

That's an excellent question, and I wouldn't be honest if I gave you a simple answer. The will to survive in the face of danger is a trait many of us share, regardless of whether we believe in God. Sure, my survival instincts came into play. However, I didn't experience the peace of God until I put everything in his hands and asked that his will be done. The peace I felt was instantaneous.

I've never heard God speak to me in an audible voice, but that afternoon, I heard his voice as clearly as if I were standing with Moses at the top of Mt. Sinai. All the fear and anxiety I carried with me into the ER just melted away because I knew, beyond a shadow of a doubt, that God was still in control.

CHAPTER V

Diagnosis Confirmed

I finally saw a doctor around 7:30 P.M.

"Mr. Brown, I'm Dr. P.," he said, extending his hand. "How are you feeling?"

"As well as could be expected, I guess," I answered.

"I've consulted a hematologist to meet with you as soon as the orderly takes you to your room," he said. "Have you had anything to eat yet?"

"No, I'm starving," I replied.

"Okay," he said. "We'll put in a call to the kitchen and get them to bring you a meal when you're settled in for the evening. Is there anything else we can do for you before then?"

"Yeah, I need to call my parents and let them know what's happening," I said.

"We'll arrange that for you as soon as possible," he assured me.

"That would be great," I said. "How long will it be before I'm admitted?"

"The nurses are cleaning your room and making the bed as we speak," he said.

Finally! This ER bed is uncomfortable.

I faced my first night in the hospital since my tonsillectomy at the age of five. Born with small eustachian tubes, I suffered from numerous ear infections and became well-acquainted with hospitals as a small child. My adenoids were removed at the age of two, and I had tubes placed in my ears three times before the age of four. My most enduring image from that time is laying on the operating table and screaming for my parents as a surgeon placed a gas mask over my face. I hated hospitals. I hated the food, the sickness, the dying, and that pungent, antiseptic smell! When I visited my mom after her operation for her deviated septum 12 years earlier, the smell was so choking that I wanted to vomit.

An orderly took me up to my room at 8:00 p.m. While I made some small talk with the nurses in charge of my care, the hematologist came in and introduced himself.

"Hello, Mr. Brown," he said. "I'm Dr. F., the hematologist on-call this evening."

"Nice to meet you," I said.

"I've had a chance to examine your latest blood results, and they show an abnormally large number of white cells in your peripheral bloodstream," he said.

"Do you think I have leukemia?" I asked.

"That's a strong possibility, but we can't tell from the blood results alone," he replied. "We'll have to do a bone marrow aspiration and biopsy tomorrow morning to determine a diagnosis. Do you have any family in the area?"

"No," I answered. "I'm a graduate student at Biola University over in La Mirada. My permanent address is at my parents' home in Virginia."

"I'll call your parents and alert them of your condition," he said. "Hopefully, I can persuade them to fly out to Los Angeles as soon as possible. Can you give me their number?"

"Sure," I replied.

After he jotted down their number, he put in an order for me to receive two units of blood and left to call my parents. A few minutes later, they were connected to my room extension.

"Hello . . . Mom?" I asked.

"Hello, Rob. Now, don't you worry. Regardless of what you have, God is able to heal you and pull you through," she said.

Just as she was finishing, my dad chimed in from another extension, "Rob? This is Dad. I'm here too."

"Hi, Dad," I said in response. "I checked in here several hours ago after the nurse at the Biola health clinic told me I was dangerously anemic and may have leukemia."

"Your mother and I are going to catch a flight out to Los Angeles first thing tomorrow morning," he said. "Remember, God is in control of this situation," he assured me. "We'll call David and Brenda and our family in North Carolina as soon as we hang up. Before we leave in the morning, we'll call the church prayer chain. Don't you worry about a thing. We'll be there tomorrow afternoon."

"Rob," my mom added, "I firmly believe that you're going to be healed, no matter what the disease is. Nothing is too big for God. Not even leukemia. We're all praying for you and believing that God will be glorified. Just have faith in him."

Before hanging up, my parents prayed for me over the phone. Despite the strained relations I had with my folks, I wanted them in my corner more than anyone else in the world.

Early the next morning, one of the residents who had been on-call the previous night stopped by my room.

"How are you feeling, Mr. Brown?" he asked.

"Okay, I guess. The blood transfusions made my arm really sore. It was hard to sleep last night," I said.

"That's a common side effect with blood transfusions," he said. "But you should start to feel better, now that you've received some new blood."

"Yeah, that's what Dr. F. told me last night," I said. "Are you the intern in charge today?"

"No, I'm getting ready to go home," he replied. "Anyway, I just wanted to see how you were doing. I understand you're a student at Biola University."

"Yeah, I'm a graduate student there," I answered. "I'm studying to be a Clinical Psychologist."

"That's a great school. Several friends of mine have attended Biola," he said.

"Are you a Christian?" I asked.

"Absolutely. If not for Christ, I wouldn't be alive today," he replied. "Listen, I want you to know that if you do have a leukemia, it's a treatable one."

"That's good to know," I said.

"Whatever your diagnosis is though, you would have to admit

that right now you're a pretty sick puppy," he said.

"Yeah, I know," I said, nodding.

"Well, I've got to go now," he said. "Take care, Robert."

"Thanks," I said, encouraged by his words and amazed at how many Christians worked at this particular hospital. My nurse the previous night was a Biola alumnus (Class '82), and an acquaintance of mine from my church worked there as a surgeon.

Later that morning, Dr. F. performed the bone marrow biopsy and aspiration, a procedure in which a tiny sample of bone marrow is withdrawn from the hip via a large needle and syringe. I've subsequently been through so many of these procedures that they no longer faze me. However, this first biopsy was quite painful because my low platelet count made me susceptible to bruising. Worse yet, my hipbone was so hard that the doctor had to drill in two places to get an adequate sample.

While I was still recovering from the experience, my parents arrived from the airport. After my father went to my place of residence to notify my landlady of my condition and tie up some loose ends for me, my mom and I spent the afternoon in my room.

"Rob, last night before I went to bed, Romans 8:28 came to mind," she said. "It says, 'And we know that in all things God works for the good of those who love him, who have been called according to his purpose.'

"God has a purpose for your life, and it hasn't been fulfilled yet," she continued. "I'm convinced of it. I told our friend Lisa of your condition last night, and the first thing she said was 'That young man has a call of God on his life.' She's already called several people asking for prayer."

Several people is an understatement. Lisa called Breakthrough Ministries, a nation-wide prayer network founded by the late Catherine Marshall, a noted Christian speaker and author of several books, including *Christy,* the novel upon which the 1994-95 television series was based. In addition to the multitudes of people praying for my healing as a result of her ministry, Catherine Marshall herself ministered to me through one of her books.

"Rob," my mom said, "During our flight out here, I read *Adventures in Prayer* by Catherine Marshall. Have you ever heard of her?"

"No," I replied.

"She was married to the late Peter Marshall Sr., a well-known Presbyterian minister in Washington, D.C."

"I've never heard of him either," I said.

"Well, at one time, he was the chaplain of the U.S. Senate," she explained. "Before that, he was the head pastor at the New York Avenue Presbyterian Church in Washington, D.C. Your father and I were married in that church.

"Anyhow," she continued, "in the fifth chapter of her book, she discusses the 'Prayer of Relinquishment.'[1] When we come to God in prayer, we can't have a demanding spirit and expect him to grant our requests. We need to entrust ourselves and those we pray for to the care of God and be willing to accept the final outcome, whatever it may be."

"Well, I agree with that," I said.

"While I was reading that chapter, God impressed upon my heart the difference between faith and striving," she said. "Faith is entrusting everything to the care and wisdom of God. Striving is the attempt to get God to see things our way," she explained. "King David's reaction after Nathan prophesied that his son with Bathsheba would die as a punishment for their adultery was an example of striving.[2] David prayed and fasted after his son became ill, but remember what happened?"

"The baby died anyway," I replied.

"You know, after reading that chapter on relinquishing our needs to God in prayer, God spoke to my heart and told me that I was striving last year when I prayed for your Uncle Bill to be healed of cancer," she said. "I couldn't accept the possibility that it might be my brother's time to go, but I was wrong. God told me to release you to him, which is something I didn't do when I prayed for Bill."

"Really?" I asked.

"Yes," she said. "At that moment, I recalled Romans 8:28, the scripture he gave me last night, and I released you to his care. Since

---

[1] Catherine Marshall, *Adventures in Prayer* (Grand Rapids, MI: Chosen Books, 1975) 51-60.
[2] II Samuel 12:1-23

then, I've had perfect peace."

"God's given me peace too," I replied. "I know my time isn't up yet."

Friday morning was the first test of how much stock we put in the promise that God would make something good come out of my current situation. Shortly after breakfast, Dr. F. came to my room and reported, "The biopsy results have come back. As I feared, it's a leukemia."

The three of us listened with bated breath as he relayed the bad news. We were silent, but not shocked. Although we had hoped my condition was less serious, the results of my blood tests had shown no signs of either an infection or a non-cancerous blood disorder. Deep down, we suspected a leukemia diagnosis would be confirmed.

"So, what now?" I asked.

"The kind of leukemia you have is Acute Myelogenous Leukemia or AML, a common form of adult leukemia," he replied.[3] "There's an 80 percent remission rate, and the treatment of choice is chemotherapy. We're looking at approximately a month-long stay in the hospital that will include several transfusions of blood, platelets, and if necessary, antibiotics to defend against infections."

"How good are my chances of a permanent remission?" I asked.

"Well, that's difficult to say," he replied. "The prognosis for someone your age is better than for older adults, but not as good as children, most of whom are diagnosed with Acute Lymphocytic Leukemia or ALL.

"Approximately half of the leukemias diagnosed are acute, which means that their course is aggressive, and the other half are chronic or slow-moving," he continued. "The latter are generally seen in older patients, whereas AML is usually seen in patients your age."

"So, are my chances pretty good?" I asked.

Rubbing his chin, he answered, "Well, the younger a person is, the better the prognosis. I can't give you any promises, but due to the side-effects of chemotherapy, such as nausea, vomiting, mouth sores, and susceptibility to infection, you can expect to get worse before you get better."

---

[3] A.K.A. Acute **Myelocytic** or Acute **Myeloid** Leukemia.

I knew little about leukemia before that morning. Since then, I've discovered that most people know as much as I did. I often use the singular "leukemia" for the sake of simplicity, but in reality, the leukemias are a broad class of cancerous disorders pertaining to the white blood cells or leukocytes. Beginning in the bone marrow, the life source of the blood and lymph system, their causes are not fully known. However, factors associated with their development include: genetic abnormalities, a rare human T-cell leukemia virus, preexisting immune system disorders, prolonged exposure to harmful chemicals or ionizing radiation, and the use of certain drugs known to suppress bone marrow functioning.[4]

The acute leukemias, in particular, are characterized by an abnormal proliferation of immature white blood cells called "blasts." Because these blast cells fail to provide an immune response and interfere with the production of platelets and red blood cells, early symptoms of leukemia are anemia, weakness, lightheadedness, and increased susceptibility to infections and bruising. The latter stages of the disease are often associated with internal hemorrhaging and complications involving the kidneys, liver, and other vital organs.[5]

Without treatment, the leukemias are fatal. The chronic leukemias may go undetected for years, but their only cure is a bone marrow transplant (BMT). The acute leukemias don't always require a BMT, but their course is so aggressive that they can be fatal within a matter of weeks. Dr. F. surmised that I'd had AML, a disease which affects the class of white cells known as the granulocytes, for approximately seven weeks. This meant that my parents and I needed to make some prompt decisions about my treatment.

Dr. F. didn't want to discharge me because of my low platelet count, but we told him it was imperative that I receive treatment in the Washington, D.C. area so I could be near friends and family. He said he would reconsider if my parents found a cancer treatment center or university hospital in the DC area, but he warned us that it might be difficult because of my limited health insurance.

---

[4] National Cancer Institute, *Research Report: Leukemia, 1987 Edition* (Washington, D.C.: U.S. Dept. of health and Human Services, 1987) 1-9.
[5] National Cancer Institute, *Research Report: Leukemia, 1987 Edition* 3.

My only health insurance was a $50,000 policy offered by my school. When we purchased it two years earlier, I was a full-time student and no longer eligible for coverage under my father's insurance. Besides, I was so healthy that none of us ever anticipated the possibility that I would have to see a doctor outside of a yearly physical, bout with the flu, or automobile accident. We assumed that a major health package was unnecessary.

There was no way a $50,000 policy could cover my leukemia treatments. Even if we were able to locate a treatment facility near home, I needed comprehensive health insurance that would cover the expenses of chemotherapy and, possibly, a subsequent BMT.

We prayed that God would lead us to the right hospital and doctor, as well as give Dr. F. peace of mind over releasing me once we found an appropriate treatment center. After that, my dad went back to my place of residence to call my brother and "Maj" (a.k.a. Lt. Col. Robert E. Renz), an old family friend, to apprise them of my condition and ask them to help in the search for a treatment facility near home. Maj consulted the National Institutes of Health (NIH) in Bethesda, MD, and my dad called the American Cancer Society (ACS). David consulted the oncology department at Reston Hospital Center in Reston, VA where our former church worship leader had received treatment for brain cancer. Before long, our prayers were answered.

"Working independently from two different places in the country (VA and CA) and through two different resources (NIH and ACS), Maj and my dad found the same doctor within five minutes of each other. Dr. Z., a hematologist affiliated with the Vincent Lombardi Cancer Research Center at Georgetown University Medical Center, had just finished talking on the phone with Maj when my dad had him paged. While my dad was waiting for Dr. Z. to answer his page, my landlady, Peggy, received a call from my mom on another extension. Maj had just called my mom at the hospital to inform her that a Dr. Z. from Georgetown had agreed to accept me as a patient and was awaiting my dad's call. When Peggy's granddaughter passed the message on to my dad, he did a double take and the rest is history.

That afternoon, Dr. Z. discussed my case over the phone with Dr. F. and assured him that it would be safe to fly me home, provided that my platelets were at least 50,000 and my red blood cells were at least

25,000. With that, plans were made to discharge me the next day.

That evening, several friends of mine came by to visit me and wish me well, and one of my professors called me on the phone to let me know that he and the entire student body would be praying for my recovery. Peggy's daughter, Sharon, also visited and introduced me to a former leukemia patient who attended her church.

"Rob, I'd like to introduce you to someone who has some of my own blood [i.e., via transfusion] flowing through her. Janelle, this is Rob Brown."

"Hi, nice to meet you," she said, extending her hand forward.

"And I'm Rob's mother," my mom said smiling.

"I'm Janelle," she said, smiling in return.

"Janelle, Rob has been diagnosed with AML," Sharon said. "I think it might be helpful if he had the opportunity to talk with someone who knows what he's about to face."

"Sure," Janelle said. "Well, three years ago, at the age of 14, I was diagnosed with Acute Lymphocytic Leukemia."

"ALL," I said. "So, I take it that you're in remission now?"

"Yes," she said.

"Perhaps you can give Rob some idea of what he can expect," Sharon said.

"Well, I'll be perfectly honest with you," she began, "the first six months of my treatment was HELL," she said laughing. "They bombarded me with chemotherapy drugs that were so strong that they wiped out all of my white cells, the healthy as well as the unhealthy. For weeks, I had no way to fight infections on my own. As for the nausea and vomiting, it got so bad at times that I couldn't eat."

"I've heard it can be pretty bad," I said.

"Yeah, they provided me with medications to control it, but that didn't always work," she replied. "There are going to be some times when you won't want to eat, and you'll have to force yourself to do so. When you're going through chemotherapy, it's best to eat bland foods that are easy to get down. Don't eat foods you really like when you're going through chemo because you might dislike those foods forever," she cautioned.

"That makes sense," I said.

"In addition to regular chemotherapy, I also received radiation treatments to my spinal cord to keep the leukemia cells from invading my Central Nervous System," she said. "I don't know if you'll go through that or not, but it can be pretty rough."

"What was it like after the first six months?" I asked.

"After that first six months, I received maintenance doses of chemotherapy that were more tolerable. During that time, I could go to school and live a relatively normal life."

"Did you lose all your hair?" I asked.

"Yes. That was hard at first. When I went back to school, I often wore a hat or a scarf to cover my head until my hair grew back," she said.

"How is your health now?" my mom asked.

"I've never felt better," she said. "Chemotherapy was difficult, but it was worth it. In fact, I'm now a spokesperson for the American Cancer Society."

"That's great," my mom said.

"Having leukemia made me a much better person, and if I had the choice to live my life all over, I would choose to go through it again," she said.

Janelle's last statement echoed a sentiment I heard years earlier when Kathy, an old high school friend of mine, testified before our church youth group. A survivor of Hodgkin's Disease, Kathy said that she was thankful to God that she went through her battle with lymphoma because of what it taught her about his grace and power. When Janelle said the same thing about her disease years later, it served as a confirmation that God had a purpose in allowing cancer to invade my body. The glow on her face and the sparkle in her eyes told me all I needed to know about whether or not life existed after cancer.

CHAPTER VI

God's Sovereignty Behind the Scenes

Saturday, June 27, my parents and I thanked the nurses for their kindness, and my dad drove us to Los Angeles International Airport. Sharon, who just happened to be a registered nurse, accompanied us at Dr. F.'s insistence. After my mom and I boarded the plane, my father drove Sharon home and returned to my place of residence to pack my belongings and prepare to drive my car back to Virginia the next day.

During the flight home, the only time I've ever enjoyed the amenities of traveling first class, I spent a lot of time thinking about the battle that lay ahead of me.

"Mom, the thing I fear the most isn't dying," I said. "It's the suffering. The chemotherapy could be hell on earth."

"I know," she said. "But God wouldn't allow you to go through anything that's too much for you to bear. If he didn't think you could handle this, he wouldn't have allowed it to happen. He obviously has a purpose for it."

"I know, but I just hope it isn't as bad as I've heard," I replied. "I don't want to go through the throwing up and the mouth sores and everything else Janelle told us about."

"Well, if anyone can handle this, you can," she said. "God has a

31

call on your life, and you haven't fulfilled it yet. That's the truth, and I would stake my life on it. He wants to use this experience to mold you into the kind of person he wants you to be."

We arrived at Washington National Airport at 10:00 p.m., where David and Brenda met us at the gate. As my mom pushed me through the terminal in a wheelchair (a pre-cautionary measure due to my low platelet count), the look of concern on my brother's face said it all. I was pale, gaunt and too weak to carry my own luggage. Just two weeks earlier, we were playing side-by-side in an intra-church league volleyball game. At that time, neither of us could have known that the headache which forced me to take a break from the action signaled something far worse than fatigue.

As Brenda's car raced down Jefferson Davis Highway and passed Arlington Cemetery on my left and the Potomac River on my right, my mind flashed back to the previous Fourth of July. I was right there, on the lawn to my right, tossing a frisbee without a care in the world. My most enduring memory from that humid evening was chasing down a long pass and stretching out to snag the disk in a single, fluid motion. As I stole a glance at the Washington Monument and fired off a throw, everything seemed perfect. This year, I would be spending Independence Day in the hospital, far removed from the smell of fireworks and grilled hotdogs.

We arrived at Georgetown University Medical Center 15 minutes later, and I was taken straight to the oncology ward. As I settled in for the night, my family tried to make my room seem as close to home as possible. In addition to bringing numerous "munchies," books, and pictures of their recent wedding to place on my night-stand, David and Brenda hung a framed, life-sized photograph of our family's miniature schnauzer on the front wall. Although absent in person, Graycee remained true to her nature and captivated the attention of everyone in charge of my care.

After the admitting intern examined me, he introduced me to Dr. E., the oncology resident monitoring my case. Dr. E explained that my treatment protocol would consist of two rounds of chemother-apy, *Induction* and *Consolidation*, followed by one of three options: (a) a third round of high-dose chemotherapy; (b) *autologous bone marrow transplantation*, a BMT in which a portion of the patient's marrow is harvested during remission, purged of residual cancer cells, and reinfused into the bloodstream; or (c) *allogeneic bone marrow transplantation,* a BMT in which the patient's marrow is destroyed via chemo and radiation and replaced by that of a donor.

"Robert, one of the advantages of university hospitals like Georgetown is their dedication to researching the latest advances in medicine," Dr. E. said. "For instance, our hematology department, along with those of other prominent east coast hospitals, is currently involved in a study that evaluates the relative effectiveness of these three treatments."

"Which of the three do you think is best?" I asked.

"I believe allogeneic BMTs work at least as good as, if not better than, chemotherapy or autologous BMTs," Dr. E. answered. "But they're not always feasible or necessary.

"The agreement to take part in this study is not a precondition for receiving care here, and you're free to withdraw at any time," he continued. "If you do agree to take part in this study, you will be randomized by computer to one of these three treatments upon completion of your first two rounds of chemotherapy."

"I have another question," I interjected. "From what I heard in California, the remission rate for my leukemia is 80 percent. How many of these patients end up relapsing?"

"Within two years of treatment, almost half of all AML patients relapse," he replied.

Always wanting to know the straight skinny, I asked, "Is there any way of telling which patients will relapse and which will be cured?"

"There's never a guarantee that all of the cancer cells have been destroyed because cells that are resistant to chemotherapy often go undetected," he explained. "Unfortunately, we can't predict who will achieve long-term survival out of that original 80 percent. I'm confident we can get you into remission after just one cycle of chemo, but research has shown that without additional treatment, your odds of relapsing are greater than 90 percent."

"Okay," I said, my questions satisfied for now.

"So, Robert, would you be willing to take part in this study?" he asked.

"Sure," I said.

"Great!" he replied. "Remember, you can withdraw at any time and it won't affect the quality of your treatment. Besides, the first two phases of treatment, Induction and Consolidation, are standard protocol for all AML patients.

"Our primary goal, first and foremost, is to get you into remission," he continued. "When you're in remission, your body can rejuvenate itself so you can withstand subsequent chemo treatments."

"When will Induction start?" I asked.

"Because you were just admitted tonight, we won't be ready to start until Monday at the earliest," he answered. "The only thing we can really do tonight is tuck you in."

"I've heard a lot about the nausea and vomiting," I said. "How bad is it?"

"It's not as much of a problem now because we have effective antinausea medications," he replied. "For instance, just last year, the FDA approved a drug called *Zofran* that has revolutionized our ability to treat nausea. As a result of this drug, which is administered by IV, most patients experience very little nausea and can eat throughout the course of their treatments."

"Well, that sounds good," I said with relief.

"Upon completing your first round of chemotherapy, you're going to feel 'washed out,'" he explained. "Although you'll be susceptible to infection for at least two weeks, we plan on discharging you if your platelet levels are decent and you're not running a fever. We'll keep you on a short leash and jerk you back in here at the first sign of an infection or other complications."

We spoke a few more minutes about my medical history and then made some small talk over what I studied in graduate school and my family background. We both discovered that we had a lot in common. Like myself, he was a home-grown product of the D.C. Metropolitan area and an avid fan of the Super Bowl Champion Washington Redskins. After he left, I visited with my family for a while longer, watched a re-run of *Saturday Night Live,* and turned in for the night.

I met my hematologist, Dr. Z., the next evening. Like Dr. E., he was gracious and easy to talk with about my treatment protocol. Our conversation was a rehash of the one I had with Dr. E., but with more elaboration.

"When will my brother be tested to see if he's a compatible donor?" I asked.

"We'll be testing him this week," he answered. "There's a 25 percent chance he'll be a perfect match, but we won't know for some time."

"If he's not a match for me, will other people be tested?" I asked.

"The research protocol we're following allows for an allogeneic BMT only if you have a matching relative," he said. "We'll consider a BMT with an unrelated donor only in the event of a relapse."

At this point, I wasn't ready to think about relapsing. I was facing seven days of controlled poisoning, and I couldn't afford to waste time and energy fretting over a negative that may never come to pass. I resolved in my heart to remain optimistic and remind myself that God was calling the shots, not the medical profession.

CHAPTER VII

Round One:
A Smooth Beginning

My first week in the hospital passed with the blink of an eye. On Monday, a Hickman catheter was surgically implanted into a large vein just below my right collar bone. Consisting of three separate ports, the Hickman made my life a lot easier because chemotherapy, antibiotics, and blood products could be administered simultaneously. Better yet, both of my arms were now free, and the nurses no longer tortured my veins with endless IVs.

Wednesday, July 1, I began Induction Therapy. Consisting of the two chemotherapy drugs *Cytosine Arabinoside (Ara-C)* and *Idarubicin*, the entire seven-day treatment went much smoother than expected. I experienced some mild diarrhea, but my nausea was so negligible that I never missed a meal and felt well enough to go for walks outside my room.

Because things went so well, I expected to be discharged from the hospital the following weekend. That Friday, however, I experienced my first setback when Dr. Z. came by for his afternoon rounds.

"Rob, we've had a change of plans," he said. "I know we've talked about discharging you this weekend, but some issues have come up that are going to make that unlikely," he said.

"What's the problem?" I asked.

"Your platelets and red blood cells are extremely low, and at some point, you're going to need some transfusions," he replied. "Problem is, you don't have the health insurance to pay for home infusion services."

"Okay," I said, nodding.

"Now, if you were discharged in the middle of the week, you could return here to receive any needed transfusions as an outpatient," he said. "Unfortunately, we were planning on discharging you this weekend, and our outpatient transfusion services are closed on Saturday and Sunday. The only way you can get transfusions over the weekend is if you're readmitted as an inpatient.

"I know you would like to get out of here, but given the circumstances, staying here is in your best interests," he explained. "Besides, your white count has become so low you could get an infection and spike a fever at any moment."

I tried to be positive, but I was disappointed. I appreciated Dr. Z.'s desire to look out for my best interests, but the walls of my room had become more confining with each day.

This disappointment aside, my experience thus far had given me a favorable impression of Georgetown University Medical Center. The oncology doctors and nurses had treated me and my family with kindness and respect from the moment I set foot on their floor. They hadn't talked down to me when I asked them questions, and most important, they always seemed positive. They couldn't guarantee a cure or even a remission for that matter, but they exuded confidence in their ability to provide me with the best possible care, regardless of my prognosis.

In addition to the compassionate care I received from the hospital staff, the support and prayers of family and friends had done much to boost my morale. Some days, especially in the beginning, I entertained visitors and talked on the phone nonstop. The intern monitoring my care remarked one morning that he'd never seen a patient have so many visitors or receive so many cards and letters, all of which I planned to save and put in three-ring binders after I was discharged.

As for my family, what can I say? They were the ones whom I counted on the most for support. Every day, my mom had stayed with me from the late morning until early afternoon, and my dad had come by after work. David and Brenda, who had moved in with my parents the previous week to save money and help around the house while I was in the hospital, had come by several times as well to lighten the mood with an endless supply of humorous anecdotes on their first year of married life. They now served as my lifeline to the outside world by updating our Sunday school class on my condition and keeping me abreast of how all my friends were spending the summer.

I couldn't help but wonder how cancer patients who have little or no support from others are able to fight their disease. Although I've had a loving family and several good friendships throughout my life, I was just now learning how much people cared about me.

During my prolonged stay in the hospital, I spent a lot of time mulling over what direction my life might take after my treatments were completed. The events of the past two weeks had turned my life upside down and forced me to confront the harsh reality that life was unpredictable and unfair. Case in point: the healthiest person I knew, myself, had just been diagnosed with cancer. I needed to focus on getting better, but feelings of insecurity and uncertainty over the direction my life would take once the treatments were over haunted me. I had no timetable for when my health would return to normal. I worried about how the outside world might perceive me and what limitations might be placed on me because of my diagnosis.

When I shared these feelings with my brother and brought up the option of changing careers, he said, "Rob, you've just been through something traumatic," he said. "Don't start making any plans until you're further along in your recovery and you've processed everything that's happened."

He was right. I needed to spend time with God and seek him for wisdom rather than make a rash decision I might regret years later. Nevertheless, I felt liberated knowing I had the option of changing my career before it was too late. I wasn't locked in to a career as a Clinical Psychologist just because I had a Master's degree, and I had no obligations to a wife or children.

Regardless of what God led me to do, I vowed that from now on, I would no longer be so self-absorbed that I missed the opportunity to demonstrate the same compassion to others that friends and family were showing me now. I wanted my post-leukemia life to be different.

CHAPTER VIII

Seven Days of Hell

<hr>

On July 14, Dr. Z. came by during his afternoon rounds and said, "Well, congratulations! As of today, you have completely 'bottomed out.' You have no white cells."

"Really? Well, I still feel pretty good," I responded with a smile.

Brenda, who was there with me, said, "Hey, Rob! If you feel so good, why don't we go outside and play a game of one-on-one?"

We all laughed. I wasn't ready to meet anyone on the court, no matter how well I felt. The chemotherapy had left me defenseless against the onset of an infection or virus. Now I wore a face mask whenever I ventured outside my room, and the hospital excluded fresh fruit and vegetables from my diet. When my friend Rob called the next day to see if he and his fiance Leslie could come over, I declined because Leslie had a cold.

Several hours after Rob's call, my health took a turn for the worse. What began as a mild sore throat developed into a high fever and a splitting headache. During the course of the night, I took *Tylenol* twice, and it did squat. I might as well have taken sugar pills. Sometime around 3:00 a.m., I pushed my call button to ask my nurse if she had anything stronger. After several minutes of waiting, she was nowhere to be found.

Why isn't she answering my call? They're usually pretty efficient here.

I called once more, and her voice finally crackled over the speaker near my bed.

"What is it, Mr. Brown?" she asked, sounding annoyed.

"I know you gave me some Tylenol an hour or so ago, but it's not helping me," I said.

"I've given you Tylenol twice already," she said.

"Well, it's not working," I retorted. "It hasn't done a thing. Can't you give me some *Advil?*"

"The Tylenol is supposed take care of it!" she huffed.

Well, it's not taking care of it! And don't argue with me about my symptoms, and what should or shouldn't take care of it. I'm the one with the headache!

Now, I was angry. I was tempted to give her a piece of my mind, but my better senses prevailed. As a group, the nurses had been wonderful, and I didn't want to ruin my rapport with any of them. It's possible that they were understaffed that evening, and my nurse felt pulled in eight directions.

I went the rest of the night without sleep. By the time my day nurse came by to take my morning vital signs, I felt horrible.

Shortly after breakfast, I went down to radiology to have head X-rays taken to rule out any neurological causes for my headache. During the procedure, they maneuvered my head around in so many directions, I became nauseous and vomited all over myself. I would have just sat there all soiled if a passing nurse hadn't done a double-take and grabbed a towel and bedpan.

Concerned that I contracted a hospital-based infection, Dr. Z. informed me later that afternoon that I would be administered round-the-clock IV antibiotics until my white counts returned to normal. "We're going to start with *Fortaz* and *Vancomyacin*," he said. "Both of these drugs are very effective with hospital-based infections."

"Can you give me anything stronger for my headache?" I asked.

"Well, I heard you asked for *Ibuprofen* last night," he said. "We can't give you that because it's notorious for causing ulcers and other gastric problems. Because your platelets are so low, it would put you at risk for abdominal bleeding."

"Well, the Tylenol isn't helping," I said, trying to be as polite as possible.

"Rob, if you were to rate your headache on a scale of 1-10, with 10 being the worst, how would you rate it?" Dr. Z. asked.

"A 9 or 10. It throbs at the front of my head and the pain shoots all the way to the back of my neck. It's unbearable," I said.

"Are you feeling dizzy too?" he asked.

"Yes," I replied.

"I'll write an order for you to receive *Percocet* to help you with your pain. If that doesn't work, we can give you *Morphine*."

"Thanks," I said.

The next week was **hell**.

For several days, I felt so sick that I stayed in bed and saw no one outside of my family and some pastors from our home church, Christian Fellowship Church (CFC), who came by to pray for me. I had trouble holding anything down, and my headache was so severe that I kept my lights off and my door closed. The sound of people talking was intolerable.

Every day, my parents, David, and Brenda took shifts staying by my bedside to let me know they were with me if I needed anything. All four of them, at one time or another, spoon-fed me cottage cheese or apple sauce because sitting up to eat made me dizzy and nauseous. Nothing put me more at ease than when one of them read the Bible to me. Listening to God's Word was the only way I could preoccupy myself with something other than my misery.

Nothing relieved my pain. Morphine, Percocet, and Tylenol with *Codeine* merely dampened it and kept me in a narcotic stupor. One afternoon, my Aunt Pat and Uncle Joe stopped in to see me enroute from Ohio to Florida, and I was so groggy I couldn't carry on a simple conversation. Another time, Pastor Ahlemann, Senior Pastor of CFC, came by to pray for me while I was asleep. When I woke up after he left, I asked Brenda, "Did Ed McMahon just come by and tell me I won ten million dollars?" I was serious! For some reason, my subconscious mind heard "Ahlemann" and interpreted it as "McMahon." Brenda laughed and replied, "No, I would have woke you up for that."

The following Monday afternoon, I continued to deteriorate. After several days on IV antibiotics, which now also included *Penicillin* and *Amphoteracin B* (an antifungal medication), my fever had climbed to 105 degrees Fahrenheit, and large bags of ice were placed by my sides to cool me down while I tried to sleep.

Tried is the operative word. Narcotic drugs will put you in a "twilight" state, but they don't induce a long, peaceful sleep. After six days of twilight, I had no frustration tolerance whatsoever. At one point, my dad upbraided me for being rude to one of the nurses.

"Rob, I know you're sick, but don't take it out on them," he said. "You're being abrasive, and you need to knock it off! I haven't said much, but you've been shouting orders at people all evening. Now, there's no reason for it. We're doing the best we can."

"I know, I know!" I said. "I'll apologize later."

My blood cultures indicated that I had a strep infection, but my high fever and headache had persisted for so long that by Tuesday, July 21, the oncology team began to suspect I might have spinal meningitis. In order to rule out such a possibility, they prepared to give me a spinal tap and put me through an oral mental status exam to test my short-term memory.

My father was so distraught over my condition that he privately cried out to God on my behalf. The Lord answered him during his morning shower:

Why do you despair, my child? Am I not in control? I say unto you that I will totally and completely heal your son."

My dad saw no flashing light and heard no audible voice, but at that moment, he knew God had spoken these words to his heart. He didn't share this experience with anyone and subsequently forgot about it until the next day when he received a note in the mail from our long-time friend Ruth. In her note, Ruth included a "word of knowledge" that God had given her in her morning prayer time that was virtually identical to the impression my dad received a day earlier! After he read Ruth's note, my dad became so excited that he typed it out in large letters and placed it on my front wall to the right of Graycee's picture.

The next evening, I took a turn for the better. The doctors were at a loss as to whether my headache was caused by my strep infection or something else. Every test had come out negative for neurological problems, including meningitis. Having exhausted all other prospective diagnoses, the doctors finally considered the possibility of an old-fashioned migraine. They gave me an IV dose of *Ergotamine*, a powerful pain reliever that has since been banned by the FDA for it's side effects, and my brain felt as if someone had doused it with a garden hose. Within seconds, I was out for the night.

When I woke up the next morning, my headache was gone, my nausea had subsided, my temperature was normal, and I began eating like a horse. When my doctors came by for their daily rounds and saw me reclining in the chair and devouring a lollipop, their mouths dropped wide open. I saw Dr. M., the intern who had been in charge of my care for the past month, and I gave him an enthusiastic thumbs up as if to say, "We did it!"

Over the weekend, my white cell count returned to normal, and I started taking walks around the hospital without wearing a mask. Although I still experienced some hazy vision and lightheadedness, I felt wonderful. Best of all, I could eat anything I wanted. That Sunday night, I treated myself to a steak dinner from Sizzler, courtesy of my mom.

The following Monday, an oncology resident performed a bone marrow biopsy to determine if I were now in remission. To be honest, I didn't know what to expect. My conviction that God would heal me wasn't going to stand or fall on this one biopsy, but I was unsure of how well I would hold up emotionally if the results still tested positive for leukemia. Throughout the day, I tried to bolster my faith by praying and meditating on scriptural promises of divine healing that my mom had typed out on 3x5 index cards.

The moment of truth arrived the next day when Dr. Z. came by for his afternoon rounds. I had been waiting on pins and needles for the past 24 hours, and the first words out of his mouth were, "The results haven't come back yet."

"When will they be available?" I asked, feigning patience to the best of my ability.

"The biopsy should be completed within the next day or so," he said.

"Do you think I'm in remission?" I asked.

"I can't tell you for certain, but your preliminary blood work looks good," he said.

Well, that's small comfort. If I'm not in remission, I probably won't get to go home. Even if he does let me go home, it'll only be for a few days. He'll want me back next week to go through this crap all over again.

Having no choice but to wait, I decided to grin and bear it. *God, I know you're in control of this thing, but I hate waiting. It seems like I always have to wait for the important things.*

CHAPTER IX

Triumphant Homecoming

"The bone marrow looks great!" Dr. Z. said as he came by my room, just an hour after he told me the results were pending.

"Really?" I asked.

"Yes," he said. "I just came back from the hematology lab, and it looks like we have a textbook remission."

"Great!" I said.

"Now, we haven't seen the final results of the spongy marrow tissue, but the aspirate, the liquid part of the marrow, shows a remission," he explained. "That's what we consider most important because it shows how your marrow is functioning at the present time. I believe the final biopsy will confirm what I've told you."

When he told me the good news, I felt like bouncing off the walls. All the trials I'd experienced the past five weeks paled in comparison to the way I felt now. I'd just stared death in the face and walked away triumphant. I've never felt such a rush of joy, and I'm not sure I ever will again until I hear the word "Yes" after I pop the question to the woman of my dreams.

When I was discharged from the hospital on Thursday, July 30, everyday things I once took for granted now seemed irreplaceable. I'd missed the droning of a lawn mower across the street, the warmth of a summer breeze, and the feel of the grass on my bare feet. Even my house took on a new aura. I'd walked through that door thousands of times before, never giving thought to the possibility that each time might be my last ever. I recalled the last time I passed through that door in early June. I was headed back to California to resume my life as a graduate student, and I didn't expect to return until late December.

What a difference seven weeks makes!

When I stepped into the house, the cool, air conditioned air caught me off guard.

Boy, I'm weaker than I thought.

"Are you keeping the house colder than normal, Mom?" I asked.

"No," she replied. "It's 72 degrees, Rob. You want your robe?"

"Yeah. It's kind of drafty in here," I said. "Can you get it for me?"

"Sure," she said.

"Hi, Rob," Brenda said, as she was coming down the stairs. "Hey Graycee, look who it is," she said.

"Hey, Brenda," I said and turned my attention to the dainty schnauzer who had just trotted into the foyer. Instead of jumping up on me and squealing with delight, Graycee hesitated and crouched down on her hind legs.

I thought she'd be going crazy. What's with her?

"Hi, Graycee!" I said. "Did you miss me?"

She studied me for a moment to see who this scanty-haired, scrawny stranger was, and satisfied it was me, she came over and let me scratch behind her ears.

Dogs have a sixth sense about things. Perhaps she smelled the chemotherapy that lingered in my system. I don't know. From the moment I walked in the door, she just "knew" I wasn't myself and approached me with caution.

Graycee wasn't alone. The joy over my remission aside, I had a long way to go before I would even **feel** like myself. I'd lost only eight pounds in the hospital, but I was 20-25 pounds lighter than before the disease. My clothes hung on me like a scarecrow. All appearances of strength and stamina had vanished. I lacked the strength to help my mom unpack the car, and I struggled to climb the stairs.

When I visited Dr. Z. the following Monday, I told him I still felt weak and lightheaded. He explained that I would feel weak for quite some time because I was anemic and underweight. "Over time, your blood results should return to normal," he said. "Right now, I'm more concerned about your liver. It's become inflamed from all of the IV medications you received."

"Is this a serious health problem?" I asked.

"The liver's a resilient organ, and it should repair itself over the next few weeks, provided you drink plenty of fluids and refrain from using painkillers and antihistamines," he replied. "We'll delay Consolidation until your liver returns to normal. Take advantage of your time home by 'stuffing' yourself with food and getting plenty of exercise and fresh air."

I had no problem carrying out Dr. Z.'s first order. Compared to hospital food, everything else is a fine dining experience. I paid no attention to fat or calories because I needed all the protein I could get to withstand my next round of treatments. McDonald's simplified things for me with their "Two Big Macs for Two Dollars" promo.

Exercise was difficult, especially in the beginning. While I was in the hospital, I stayed in bed so long that my legs were reduced to matchsticks. When my friend Heather and I went for a walk in my neighborhood a few days after I came home, we quickly abandoned the idea because I lacked the energy and leg strength to go uphill for long stretches.

During my furlough home from the hospital, I spent as much time as possible with friends and family. In addition to Sunday Brunches and excursions to Burke Lake and the Warrenton Air Show, I entertained visitors in our home and went out to dinner several times. Nothing else, outside of loving God and feeling healthy, mattered. I had just left behind a network of friends in California who had become like family to me. I had several friends at church, but I'd always felt so drawn toward the future I was building at Rosemead that I never set down any roots. Now I was tied to Virginia for the foreseeable future, and I needed to reconnect with my church peers more than ever.

Fortunately, David and Brenda, who met each other at church two years earlier, were still key members of the Singles' group leadership team. In fact, David had been interning as a lay minister under Kelley, our Singles Pastor, for the past year. One reason people at CFC had been so supportive of me was because of their affection and respect for my brother. The day I returned to Sunday School, several people rushed toward me with open arms, telling me I was a "walking miracle" and that they had prayed for me every day.

Over the next three weeks, other friends treated me the same way. It seemed as if the entire world had been pulling for me to beat my illness. I wasn't used to this kind of attention, and it embarrassed me. I'd just been through an ordeal I wouldn't wish on my worst enemy, but I still wanted to be seen as normal.

At church, I became an instant celebrity because of my diagnosis. Outside the church, I just stuck out. Before my diagnosis, I had thick, wavy brown hair. Although I retained some of it, I shaved it off when I got home so my baldness would look natural. My friend Heather told me I looked good bald, but reality hit home when a little girl pointed at me and asked her mom, "Is there something wrong with him? Why doesn't he have any hair?" All I could do was laugh and say, "It's only temporary."

A week before I returned to the hospital for my second round of treatments, I met the mother of a fellow leukemia patient who had no reason to laugh. I'd just seen Dr. Z. for a routine appointment that morning, and my dad and I were eating lunch in the cafeteria when a middle aged woman with blond hair and thick glasses came over and introduced herself.

"Well, I can tell you're doing well," she said.

"Yeah, I'm in remission now," I said. "I'll be returning for Consolidation next week. By the way, this is my dad."

"Dave Brown. Nice to meet you," my dad said, as he extended his hand forward.

"You're a very lucky young man," she commented. "What's your diagnosis?"

"AML," I replied.

"My daughter, Monica, has ALL," she said. "She went through two rounds of chemo and failed to go into remission. She went through a BMT earlier this summer as a last resort."

"How's she doing?" I asked.

"Not well," she replied, shaking her head. "She's developed pneumonia in both lungs, and she's on a respirator in the ICU."

"I'm sorry to hear about that," my dad said.

"How old are you?" she asked me.

"I'm 24," I answered. "How old is Monica?"

"She's 26, and she just got married this past year. I don't know how much longer she'll be with us," she said, choking up with emotion. "Her doctor has just about given up hope."

"Is it all right if we pray for you and your daughter?" my dad asked.

"Sure, by all means, do," she said, nodding.

"Let's pray," my dad said. "Remember, doctors can treat illness, but God is the healer."

With that, the three of us bowed our heads and prayed for her daughter. We put Monica's name on the church prayer chain that week and called the hospital later that summer for an update on her condition, but the staff told us she was no longer there. I never found out what happened to Monica, but short of a miracle, she probably died. I often think about her, and I'm sorry our paths never crossed. As I prepared for my second round of treatments, her story served as a painful reminder that no matter how bad things seemed, they could always be worse. Like her mother said, I was very fortunate. And, I might add, very blessed.

CHAPTER X

Round Two

I returned to Georgetown on Monday, August 17. Although I was still in a weakened condition, I finally had the energy to go for long walks around my neighborhood, I'd regained the weight I lost during Induction, and my color had returned to normal.

Dr. Z. was elated with my progress, but he tempered his pleasure because many AML patients who go into remission eventually relapse. Although it's difficult to determine which patients are at a high risk for relapse, chromosomal abnormalities are often a common factor. The week before I returned to the hospital, Dr. Z. told me that my blast cells had a chromosomal abnormality at the time of my diagnosis. "I'll be candid with you," he said. "I'd rather you didn't have this, but since we still have so much to learn about leukemia, it's difficult to give you a prognosis."

"Is this abnormality something I've always had, or was it caused by the disease?" I asked.

"I wish I could provide you with a good answer, but I can't," he replied. "But you're young, you have a good baseline health, and your leukemia responds well to chemotherapy. Those are all factors in your favor."

This wasn't good news, but I'd come too far to forget that my trust needed to be in God alone. Dr. Z. didn't have all the answers, and even if he did, it wouldn't have improved my prognosis. My source of comfort needed to be my relationship with God, and my faith in him was bolstered by a phone conversation with an old friend.

Melanie and Ron R. have been friends of mine since the late '80s. Ron and I shared duties playing drums with the church worship team during my senior year of high school, and David and I were both members of their wedding party in August 1989. During my time in CA, Melanie often called me to encourage me in my faith and to request prayer for Ron and her family. Melanie, like my mom, can discern trouble long before it becomes apparent to the average person.

Two weeks before my diagnosis, Melanie left a cryptic phone message at my CA residence urging me to call her as soon as possible. I'm usually good at returning calls, but I was so wrapped up in nailing down my academic schedule for the coming semester that her call slipped my mind. Two months later, I called Ron and Melanie to tell them I was in remission and to thank them for visiting me in the hospital. During the course of our conversation, I recalled her phone call and asked her about it.

"Melanie, I forgot to call you back after you left me a phone message two months ago," I said. "I know it's a moot point now, but why were you calling me?"

"Rob, two months ago, God woke me up in the middle of the night to pray for you," she said matter-of-factly.

"Really?" I asked in astonishment.

"Yes," she replied. "I woke up with an awful feeling that something was wrong with you," she continued. "Knowing you needed my prayers, I turned to Ron and said, 'Wake up! Something is wrong with Rob Brown! We need to pray for him.'

"Ron mumbled, 'Then pray for him!' and rolled over to go back to sleep," she said, laughing. "There was no use trying to wake him again, so I called his mother, Linda. I told her the same thing, and we prayed for you without a clue as to why you needed our prayers."

"I never would have guessed that's why you called me," I said.

"Well, Rob, God does this to me sometimes," she said. "I called you the next morning to see if you were okay, but you weren't home. When David called later that month to tell us you had leukemia, I told Ron, 'Well, now I know why I've been praying for him all this time.'"

I hung up the phone, amazed at how God works. When Melanie called me in early June, I was just beginning to feel the effects of my leukemia. By the time of my diagnosis, I'd been in her prayers for two weeks! Knowing this, I returned to Georgetown, confident that he was looking out for me.

Unlike my previous stay in the hospital, I stayed in a two-bed unit and had a roommate. Bill, a retired businessman, was diagnosed with cancer of the larynx earlier that spring. From what I could see, he seemed healthy. He retained his hair, ate anything he wanted, and walked the hospital halls several times a day. As for myself, I became so sick that I couldn't keep anything down, except for saltines and ginger ale.

Consolidation should have been easier than my first round of treatments because it only lasted five days. However, I developed a high fever and a migraine that became so bad that I was moved to a private room and placed on IV antibiotics. Dr. J., the attending hematologist for that month, told me I wouldn't be discharged until my temperature returned to normal and my blood cultures showed no signs of infection. He warned me that I might remain there for a month.

The intern on-call performed a spinal tap on Thursday afternoon to rule out neurological causes for my headache, and it came back negative. I was finally given an injection of Ergotamine that evening, and sure enough, the pain was gone the next day. The nausea subsided shortly thereafter, but my fever persisted until Sunday morning. That Saturday night, I perspired so much that the nurses changed my bedsheets three separate times within a period of four hours.

My clinical picture improved so much over the weekend that my doctors surmised that my fever and headache were caused by the chemotherapy, not an infection. However, because they needed more time to draw conclusions from my blood cultures, I remained on IV antibiotics until Thursday evening. When I was finally discharged on Friday, I was past the point of tolerating hospital food. The sight of it made me want to upchuck. My dad tried eating some of it so it wouldn't go to waste, and he could barely stomach it himself.

During the five days I spent in the hospital after my fever broke, I felt well enough to venture out into the hallways and become acquainted with a number of other patients, some of whom were my age. Not only did I have a more productive outlet for passing the time away than watching reruns of *Seinfeld* and *Murphy Brown,* but I also had several opportunities to share what God had done in my life.

During one of my excursions to the sixth floor balcony, an outdoor haven and smoking lounge, one patient remarked, "You don't like wearing hospital clothes do you?"

"No, I guess not," I replied.

The average hospital gown, which opens from the back, is so thin it leaves little room for the imagination. However, my choice of clothes went deeper than my dislike of the gown. Wearing street clothes or a pajama top with sweats helped me regain a sense of control over my life. It reminded me that my present status was temporary and my disease didn't define me as a person.

The afternoon I was discharged, my hematologist laid down specific health guidelines I needed to follow to the letter. "Make sure you wear a face mask whenever you venture outdoors," he said. "You can eat anything as long as it's thoroughly cooked."

"And no fresh fruit or vegetables," I added.

"Right. And wash your hands and avoid crowds," he said.

"What about the dog?" I asked. "Should I stay away from her as well?"

"The problem with pets is that they might jump up on you, scratch you and cause an infection. I don't think you need to avoid her, but be careful," he said. "Because a fever is the first sign of an infection, I want you to call the hematology clinic if your temperature goes above 99.0 degrees Fahrenheit."

"Do you consider that a fever?" I asked, knowing my temperature fluctuates between 97 and 99 degrees when I'm healthy.

"I usually don't consider a temperature below 100.4 grounds for admittance, but I want to be alerted about all low-grade fevers," he said. "With someone in your condition, the onset of an infection can be sudden and life-threatening."

"How often should I take my temperature?" I asked.

"Three times a day," he said. "For additional protection, I've written you prescriptions for *Cipro* and *Diflucan.* Take them as instructed and make sure you visit the clinic every other day."

"Sure," I said, not wanting to jeopardize my health through my own carelessness.

Following my discharge, I spent time at home reading about my disease and learned that chromosomal abnormalities often disappear during remission.[1] Knowing I had a chromosomal abnormality in my white cells, I asked God to heal it. I made a statement of faith that in the near future, Dr. Z. would report that my chromosomes were completely normal.

Two days after I made that claim of faith, I went to see Dr. Z. When he walked into the examining room, the first words out of his mouth were, "I have good news. Your blood work shows the chromosomal abnormality in your white cells has disappeared!"

Praise God! I just prayed about this the other day!

The disappearance of the abnormality confirmed that I had achieved a stable remission. Hearing this news within two days of my statement of faith bolstered my optimism. God wasn't letting anything escape his notice.

The following evening, I developed a low-grade fever. I saw Dr. Z. early the next morning, and he said, "Well, it looks like we're going to have to bring you back in here. From what I can see from your blood results though, it looks as if it might only be for a week at the most."

"You mean my counts are already coming back?" I asked.

"Yes," he replied. "Because this round of chemotherapy was less toxic than the first, we expected your counts to come back earlier."

I remained in the hospital and received IV antibiotics for six days. During that time, the only thing that went wrong was when the Redskins laid an egg against the Cowboys on *Monday Night Football*. The evening nurse who took my vital signs during the game said, "Your blood pressure has spiked since the last time I took it. Does the game have something to do with it?"

"Probably," I sighed, thoroughly disgusted with the home team's performance.

I was discharged Friday, September 9, just after lunch time. Considering that I'd just been through two rounds of heavy chemotherapy in a span of three months, I looked and felt better than expected. A week after my discharge, I attended a wedding

---

[1] National Cancer Institute, *Research Report: Leukemia, 1987 Edition* 7.

and surprised everyone by dancing at the reception. While my friend Laurie and I were dancing, she exclaimed, "What's all this stuff about your being so ill? YOU'RE NOT SICK!" Relatively speaking, she was right, but it wasn't time to celebrate yet.

CHAPTER XI

Round Three: The End or a Delay?

As the signs of Autumn crept over the Virginia landscape, I prepared for my final round of treatments. Since David was excluded as a potential match in July, I faced either an autologous BMT or a third round of chemotherapy. Although I was relieved when the computer selected me to receive the latter because it would be less grueling, I suspected that we might be prolonging an eventual relapse. My doctors harbored their doubts as well, and they continued searching for a marrow donor as an insurance policy.

Speaking of insurance, my first round of treatments had exhausted my $50,000 college policy. Although Brenda and my dad found an insurance company several weeks into my treatments, I couldn't receive their coverage until August '93 because my disease was a "pre-existing condition." VA Medicaid and the Hill-Burton Hospital Fund had agreed to pay my present medical expenses, but neither would cover the cost of a BMT, which could easily exceed $200,000. That said, medical expenses remained a concern.

Later that summer, Wayne Libby, the Business Administrator at our church, steered us toward the National Foundation for Transplants, a non-profit, tax-exempt organization that helps organ and marrow transplant candidates raise funds to cover present and future medical expenses.[1] Due to my lack of health insurance and indigent status as a graduate student, the Foundation accepted me as a candidate. In mid-September, we assembled a 10-member committee of close friends and relatives to help us plan and oversee our fundraising endeavors. That task seemed daunting, but we left the results to God.

The odds of curing my leukemia without an allogeneic BMT weren't in my favor. Although I believed God would eventually heal me, I dreaded the possibility of his allowing me to relapse first so he could teach me something like patience. Comparing high-dose chemotherapy to a BMT with an unrelated donor is like comparing a thunderstorm to an F-5 tornado. I had a high threshold for physical suffering, but I felt like I'd already "paid my dues." I saw no logic in God's choosing not to heal me now.

Shortly before I returned to the hospital, Shirley, the mother of an old high school friend, sent me a get-well card that helped me regain my perspective. I hadn't seen or heard from her in years, but she told me God woke her up the previous night to pray for me. Although she had no idea why I was on her heart, she sensed I was troubled and needed encouragement. She gave me no word of knowledge or scripture verse that spoke to my need, but when I read her card, I received a gentle reminder that regardless of the crises that come my way, God will prove himself faithful. He could be trusted.

My final round of treatments consisted of twelve IV bags of ultra-concentrated Ara-C, and it lasted six days. The day I was admitted, Dr. Z. said, "At this dosage, Ara-C acts as if it were a different drug from the one used in Induction and Consolidation. In addition to the nausea, you might also experience "dry eyes," mouth sores, and temporary problems with your equilibrium and coordination."

"One resident told me this drug might keep my immune system down for a month," I said.

"It could take that long," he replied. "However, I had one patient who went through this treatment and managed to stay out of the hospital the entire time."

---

[1] Formerly known as Organ Transplant Fund.

"Really?" I asked.

"Yes, but that's pretty unusual," he laughed and added, "I've prescribed some eye drops to increase your tear flow and reduce the chance of infection in your eyes. Be careful not to use it more than necessary because the steroid in these drops is addictive."

"Okay," I said. "Thanks."

Dr. Z. wasn't kidding about the toxicity of my treatments. By the evening of the second day, my nausea and vomiting became so severe I required three antinausea medications just to eat.

When I was discharged on Sunday, October 11, I had a metallic taste in my mouth and persistent diarrhea for the next week. Worse yet, the antinausea medications threw my sleeping patterns so out-of-kilter that I averaged less than two hours of sleep for the first four nights I was home. One evening, I stayed up until 4:30 A.M. balancing my checkbook, figuring I might as well do something constructive. Between the leukemia and the move back home, I hadn't straightened out my finances in months.

All things considered, I managed to stay home for six days. One afternoon, Dr. Z. remarked that I was living a "charmed existence." Unfortunately, I spiked a fever the following evening and spent the next two weeks in the hospital.

Getting an infection with no immune system is dangerous, but the experience had become so "old hat" for me I was nonchalant about the whole affair. The fever was mild to moderate at worst, and it broke within 48 hours. From that time on, I passed the time watching TV, following the Clinton/Bush election, and fumbling through the *Washington Post*, the *Washington Times* and *USA Today* (I was more informed as a patient than I had ever been before my diagnosis). The experience took dullness to new heights.

A few days before I was discharged, I saw a familiar face during one of my walks through the hospital. It was Bill, my roommate two months earlier. I didn't recognize him at first because he looked so gaunt and frail.

He doesn't look so good. I hope his cancer isn't terminal.

"Hey, you're Rob, aren't you?" he asked.

"Oh yeah, I remember you," I replied. "We were roommates last summer. How are you?"

"Well, we're still at it. Since I last saw you, I went through a tracheotomy to help me with my breathing," he answered. "You're looking good. How have things been?"

"I'm just about finished with my treatments," I said, feeling guilty over the disparity between my condition and his. "I had my last round of chemo several weeks ago, and I should be out of here by the end of the week."

"That's good to hear," he said. "Take care of yourself."

"You too," I said. "And tell your wife I said 'Hello.'"

As we went our separate ways, I was struck by how much our fortunes had reversed. I wasn't out of the woods yet, but my fight with cancer was over for now. I had won my first and what I hoped would be my only battle with leukemia.

When I looked back over the past four months, I had reason to give thanks. God had demonstrated a side of his grace that can only be experienced in the dark times. When I was at my worst and felt too weak to pray, he moved countless others to intercede on my behalf and proved himself to be true to his character. The 18 days of controlled poisoning I'd endured since the first of July were as tough a chemo regimen as you'll find, short of a BMT. Lesser treatments have resulted in fungal infections, lost spleens, and kidney failure. In my case, none of my vital organs had sustained damage.

Coming to terms with the ending of my cancer treatments had its negative side as well. I'm ashamed to admit it, but I'd grown accustomed to the constant care and affection I received. The range of visitors to the hospital had tapered dramatically since my Induction treatments, but I'd remained the center of attention in my family. I was going to miss it.

Even worse than my narcissistic longing for the spotlight were the "What Now?" questions. Four months earlier, I had a goal: to get better. Now that I'd reached that goal, I didn't know what to do with myself. Soon after my discharge, I would be thrust back into a world where I was unemployed, doubting my career choice, and lacking the assurance of being cured. Once the surgeon removed my Hickman catheter and I left for home on Friday, Nov. 4, 1992, I felt a mixture of joy and apprehension. *What Now?*

CHAPTER XII

Back in the Saddle Again

<hr>

When I came home from the hospital, I just wanted life to return to normal. My ordeal with leukemia lasted 133 days, a drop in the bucket in the span of my 25 years. However, the course of my life had been completely altered. Normal no longer existed. Greeting each day without a thought to my health status had become a fantasy. Now I couldn't make plans a week in advance without acknowledging that my next blood test could throw my life back into chaos.

Five months had passed since my last final exam, and my life at Rosemead had already become a fading memory. During my first year there, the Associate Dean of Students admonished my class not to treat our graduate experience as a "parentheses" in our lives. I ignored his advice and wasted valuable time worrying about how others perceived me. Instead of living my life to the fullest and getting the most out of my education, I assumed I had five years to grow into my role as a counselor and straighten out my priorities with respect to God and family.

Leukemia proved me wrong. None of us are guaranteed the time to get our lives on track. We may think we have lots of time, but we really don't know that for sure. What we decide today about God, family, and the direction of our lives might be the last choices we make about anything. Besides, regardless of how long we're here, things don't always go as planned. Life is full of U-turns and detours.

As for myself, I didn't just need to get my life back on track. I had to recreate it with God's help. Three obstacles stood in my way: fear of relapse, loss of independence, and lack of direction.

I tried not to think about relapsing, but it always lurked in the back of my mind. Two nights before I left the hospital, I told God that if the universe were set up in such a way that I could order him to heal me now, I would have done so. The very thought was absurd, but I decided to be honest since God already knew how I felt. I wanted to trust him, but it was easier said than done.

From my "common-sense" point of view, a relapse would cost too much money, put a strain on my family, and delay my efforts to get on with my life. The final verdict rested in God's hands, and I feared that if a potential donor were found, he'd go ahead and allow me to relapse. I secretly hoped the search for a donor would fail. Sick and tired of hearing how good my chances were in finding an unrelated donor because of my Anglo-Saxon heritage, I told my parents to stop talking about it. Ignoring reality changed nothing, but facing it head-on distressed me. I wanted to live and act as if I'd been given a clean bill of health.

As my first order of business, I made wholesale changes in my lifestyle. My immune system was weakened by three rounds of chemotherapy, and I was forced to re-consider the way I treated my body. I could no longer afford to let nutrition, rest, and exercise take a backseat to momentary gratification.

As a child, my parents insisted that I ate a balanced diet and went to bed at a reasonable hour. When I went away to college and graduate school, I set the rules. Fat, fiber, cholesterol, and betacaratene meant nothing to me. My idea of a balanced diet was having a salad with dinner, avoiding whole milk, and eating breakfast twice a week. During the summer of '87, a perusal of my cancelled checks from my first year at ORU revealed that I spent more on late-night pizzas than movies and school supplies combined! "Rob, your summer job at McDonald's is nothing more than a means of financing your pizza habit during the school year," my dad quipped.

My nutritional habits went hand-in-hand with my style of time management. In college and graduate school, I made all-nighters an art form. Every time I pulled one, I vowed it would be the last. As night turns to day, however, things remained the same for six years. During that time, I never learned how to use the spellcheck on my old Visual 1050 computer. When the first draft out of the printer lands on the professor's desk 10 minutes later, proofreading it becomes an afterthought. Now my days of functioning on three hours of sleep and relying on caffeine and Frito Lay to pull me through were gone forever.

I never concerned myself with questions over fat and cholesterol during my chemotherapy treatments because I needed the extra protein to withstand its side-effects. Now that my treatments were finished, I no longer had an excuse to binge. I needed to think about what I put into my body. For the first time in my life, stuffing carrots into a juicer took precedence over dropping coins into a soda machine and fresh fruit displaced Aunt Jemima at breakfast. The adjustment was daunting, but I was willing to do anything to avoid a relapse.

A month after my discharge from the hospital, I purchased a six-month membership at the county recreation center . . . something I never would have done had it not been for the leukemia. I ran 3-4 times a week before my diagnosis, but I never fancied myself as a fitness buff. An average athlete at best, I watched sports more often than I played them. During my first year of graduate school, I put on 20 pounds.

I often talked about joining a health club and starting a weight training program, but my excuses were always the same:

I'm too busy with school and can't find the time to go to the gym.
I can't afford those monthly fees.
I'll feel out of place there because I don't look like a bodybuilder.

I played this charade to perfection, but the bottom line wasn't money or ego. I wanted to get in shape, but I lacked the discipline to work for it. Now I had the chance to reverse that trend, and I wholeheartedly threw myself into it. The day after my first trip to the gym, I hurt so badly I had trouble putting on my sports jacket without assistance.

My poor body image was almost as large a health-related issue as my fear of relapse. The chemotherapy eroded all semblance of muscle tone from my body. For months, I wore loose T-shirts and sweats to the gym because I didn't want anyone to see how frail I looked. As with most cancer patients, my hair was completely gone. Some of my friends tried to reassure me that most people assumed I was in the military. That mistake may have been possible from a distance, but just one look at my fragile physique and the bags under my eyes set the record straight.

My career goals concerned me as much as my health. I thought I'd settled this issue years earlier, but now everything was in flux. Due to my high risk of relapse, returning to Rosemead or applying into another doctoral program was out of the question. I was tied to the D.C. area indefinitely. Besides, I didn't even know if I wanted to be a counselor. I had interests in other professions such as Law, Journalism, and Teaching, but as I evaluated my options, I became angry and dejected. Changing careers midstream would involve several more years of schooling, training, and student loans.

The M.A. I worked so hard to achieve now seemed worthless. As a professional student, I had few marketable skills outside my field of study. My knowledge of business, economics, electronics, and computers could have fit into a thimble. When I walked down the aisle as an Honors student at ORU two years earlier, my future looked bright and full of promise. Now I fought pangs of jealousy over my peers who had become established in their careers and moved out of their parents' homes.

I always assumed I'd be out on my own by my mid to late 20s, but due to economic and medical reasons, I was back to living with my parents. I felt as if my circumstances had stripped away my adulthood and catapulted me back to adolescence. I had to live by someone else's rules and be accountable to someone else for my actions. My parents respected my independence, but now they had ample opportunity to question the wisdom of all of my decisions, not just some of them. Issues such as when I ate my meals, watched TV, or went out with friends became subjects for debate. Although I loved my parents and felt closer to them than before my diagnosis, our four-month honeymoon was over by Thanksgiving. We fell into the same relationship patterns that caused a rift between us before, and I wanted to jump out of my skin.

Our first major argument occurred in mid-November. A friend and I had made plans to go dancing with a couple of single women we met at church. My parents voiced no qualms about dancing as long as it's done with good taste, but they had major reservations about us going to a sports bar or night club.

"Well, are you going to a restaurant with a dance floor or a singles' bar that happens to serve food?" my mom asked.

Here it comes.

"I don't know. What difference does it make?" I asked. "I'm not going there to 'pick up' someone."

Mom's going to get on her moral high horse and tell me I shouldn't go there because of the atmosphere, the clientele, and the possibility that someone who knows I'm a Christian might see me and be offended or led astray.

"Look Rob, I'm not against your dancing," she said. "One of the first things that attracted me to your dad was that he was a good dancer. But things have gotten worse since we dated. Most sports bars and night clubs are a magnet for alcoholics and people who try to force themselves on women. I don't think you have any business going there."

While she was still talking, my dad walked in and asked, "What's this commotion about?"

"Nothing!" I shouted, not wanting to bring my dad into the discussion.

"Dave, tell me if I'm being unreasonable," my mom said as I sighed and rolled my eyes.

"I don't have a problem with Rob wanting to go dancing," she continued, "but I don't like the idea of him taking someone to one of those 'pick-up bars.'"

"It's not a pick-up bar," I retorted.

"Absolutely not," my dad said flatly. "I agree with your mother. Singles' bars are not the place where you should be taking a date. Take my word for it. People who frequent those bars are looking to 'shack up' for the evening."

"Dad," I interjected, "I'm just going there with a girl I met at church."

"Rob, it's not you I'm worried about," he said. "It's the other people there. What if some guy cuts in on you while you're dancing and picks a fight?"

"That's not going to happen, Dad," I said.

"How do you know?" he asked. "Rob, if I were the father of this girl you're taking out, I wouldn't let her go near you again if you took her to one of those places."

"Have you prayed about your decision to go to this place?" my mom asked.

"Mom, don't give me that!" I snapped.

"Well, have you?" she asked.

"No, I shouldn't have to," I replied. "I just decided to do it."

"**Always** pray about everything," she said.

"Rob, we're not trying to cramp your style," my dad added. "We're really not."

Our arguments often progressed this way. I resented their unsolicited advice, and I accused them of being over-protective, especially in matters related to my health. My mom and I butted heads for months over how I "dragged my feet" on meeting with the Georgetown BMT coordinator for an update on their donor search. I also thought she went overboard in her concern about the alleged link between cancer and EMFs (i.e., Electromagnetic Fields):

"Rob, Don't stand so close to the juicer! You should be a minimum of two feet away from it."

"Don't use electric razors or hair dryers. They've been linked to cancer."

"Don't stand in front of the microwave! How many times do I have to say it?"

Every time she uttered these kinds of statements, my blood just boiled.

In all fairness to Mom and Dad, my transition from graduate student to leukemia survivor wasn't easy for anyone. They went from having the home to themselves to sharing space with two other distinct family units: me, a single adult; and David and Brenda, who were virtual newlyweds. Our household consisted of three systems trying to function as one without losing their separate identities. Everyone had to adapt to accommodate the needs of four other adults.

I bore the responsibility for many of our arguments. For instance, I reserved the right to go dancing wherever I wanted, and my parents weren't going to stop me. But I also knew that freedom and responsibility go hand-in-hand. Since I didn't pray about or think through my plans, I couldn't answer their concerns. Left with no alternative, I argued with them.

Shortly thereafter, I began seeing a Christian therapist to discuss my relationship with my parents and process my feelings about cancer, graduate school, and the uncertainty of my career goals. During the course of my first session with him, I discovered I had unrealistic expectations of both of my parents, especially my dad. I resented him for his temper when I was younger, and I'd kept it locked away as an adult. He'd changed for the better, but it was never good enough. When my therapist asked me if I expected him to be as patient, loving, and all-knowing as God, a light went on in my head. I'd never thought of it in that way.

I hold my dad to a standard I can't adhere to myself.

As for my mom, I resented her less, but argued with her more often. My main beef with her was that, from my perspective, she tried to be the Holy Spirit and function as my conscience. I respected her advice and often ate crow when she proved me wrong, but I just wished all my decisions weren't subject to her review. I longed for the day when I didn't have to answer to anyone. Deep down, I knew I would always be accountable to someone, whether it's my parents, God, a supervisor, or my future wife. No matter how hard I try, I can't avoid it.

Counseling helped me recognize that the leukemia had done me a huge favor. It gave me a second chance to address some key issues in my relationship with my parents that I'd swept under the rug. When I left for California, I tried to cut the cord without attempting to resolve my points of contention with them. I shared this with my therapist one day, and he said, "Rob, many people do that, but unlike them, you have an opportunity to repair the emotional damage."

I nodded in agreement.

"If you take advantage of it," he continued, "you'll be able to cut that cord later without spoiling your future relationship with them or your own kids."

"That's true," I said.

As a result of therapy and my own soul-searching, I chose to continue pursuing a career in counseling. I took an inside look and concluded that when all was said and done, I was wired to be a therapist. I loved helping people and had been a natural at offering a listening ear or an encouraging word since childhood. My inexperience and floundering relationship with God had been the reasons I doubted myself, and I knew I'd never be happier doing anything else.

Unsure of how to break into the mental health field, I met with a friend of Maj's who was a Licensed Psychologist. Upon learning I could earn a living without a doctoral degree, I set my sights on becoming a Licensed Professional Counselor (LPC). That spring, I registered with the VA Board of Professional Counselors and Marriage and Family Therapists as a post-graduate trainee, and I enrolled in a continuing studies program at nearby Marymount University (Arlington, VA) to complete the additional courses I needed for licensure.

Since I couldn't work full time without losing my Security Supplemental Income (SSI) and health coverage through VA Medicaid, my therapist suggested that I volunteer my services for some of the community mental health organizations in the area to gain hands-on experience. I took his advice, and by March, I was cofacilitating a weekly parenting class with a nonprofit counseling agency in Falls Church, VA and working 15-20 hours a week as a Volunteer Case Manager/Intake Counselor with Alexandria Mental Health Center (AMHC) in Alexandria, VA. AMHC provided me with one hour of face-to-face supervision with a Licensed Clinical Social Worker (LCSW) for every six hours of direct service to clients. I received no pay for my services, but every hour counted toward my LPC requirements.

I approached Memorial Day '93 confident my life was finally headed in the right direction. After months of working on my relationship with my parents, we'd reached a happy medium with one another. All three of us made an effort to communicate without assuming hidden motives or interrupting one another.

In the course of living under the same roof again, my dad and I discovered we're alike in as many ways as we're different. We agree on politics, we can't help yelling at the Redskins when they blow a play or get flagged for a penalty, we get so invested in projects that we forget everything else around us, and we have very precise tastes when it comes to buying clothes or appliances. When my mom took me shopping at Hecht's for a leather jacket one afternoon, she just stood there and laughed at how many jackets I tried on before I found the right one.

"You're definitely your father's son. No question about that," she said.

"What do you mean?" I asked. "Did he do the same thing when he bought his jacket?"

"Yes! He was exactly like you," she replied. "They're all the same style of jacket, made by the same company. But you and your dad are: 'This one's too stiff,' 'The zipper doesn't work right on that one,' 'This one's too soft,' and on and on and on," she laughed.

"Yeah, I guess we're more alike than I thought," I said.

True to form, he chose a stiff, hard jacket, and I chose one with a softer, more flexible feel to it. To this day, we don't like switching jackets, even though they're the same size and brand. Over that past year, God brought several friends into my life to fill the void I experienced from leaving California. I became involved in two singles' groups: my home church group, "Single Diversity," and "Career Fellowship," an interdenominational group of 300-plus singles in their 20s and 30s that met every Sunday night at McLean Presbyterian Church in McLean, VA. I also participated in two home care groups, one of which was with my parents (Gasp!). Some of my best friends today belonged to those two home groups.

My relationship with God had grown closer as well. Instead of leaning upon my own wisdom, I now sought him daily for guidance and strength. The results were far superior. The staff at AMHC gave me the green light to begin training as a Volunteer Emergency Services/Crisis Counselor in late May, and my supervisor told me she wanted to start refering clients to me for individual and group therapy. For the first time since my senior year at ORU, I was excited about becoming a therapist. When I began my first class at Marymount, I hung onto every word my professor said, even when he reviewed stuff I already knew.

My health and stamina were fabulous. Dr. Z. himself said that I looked as if I'd never had leukemia. My hair had grown back thicker and curlier than ever. When I visited the nurses on the oncology floor in early May, they all raved over how well I looked. So did my relatives when I attended my cousin Angie's wedding on Memorial Day weekend. In the best shape of my life, I'd virtually doubled my strength after six months of training with the Nautilus equipment at the County Rec Center. Everything seemed to be going my way until the second week of June.

CHAPTER XIII

The Indian Summer
Has Ended

Since I participated in a research study on AML patients, I underwent a bone marrow biopsy every other month. Until my June biopsy, they had all been completely normal. I was as healthy as the next person, and outside of a cold that past December, I hadn't been sick since my last chemo treatment. Kelley, the Minister of Single Adults at my church, called me the "Miracle Single." Despite how well things were going, however, I approached my biopsy on June 7 with some trepidation. Some cancer patients "know" they've relapsed before the symptoms become apparent. That was me.

My appetite was great, I'd lost no weight, and I was still going to the gym 3-4 times a week, but something didn't seem right. Around Memorial Day Weekend, I noticed that my heart pounded harder during my workouts, and I frequently experienced headaches after a long day at the office. I first attributed these symptoms to my busy schedule and "pollen season." After all, I'd spent most of my free time the past two months doing yard work for my parents.

I'm going to have to stop worrying about a relapse every time my eyes look bloodshot and I feel light-headed and tired. Can someone who has leukemia go full-force for thirty minutes on the Stairmaster and then lift weights for an hour? I don't think so.

I tried to deny its existence, but the suspicion that my leukemia had returned lurked in the back of my mind. A week before my biopsy, I began meditating on the healing scriptures that inspired me the previous summer just to allay my doubts.

In months past, I usually had to call the hematology office a few days after a biopsy to find out the results. The day after my June biopsy, Dr. Z. called **me** and left a message requesting that I call him about my results. In keeping with the age-old adage that no news is good news, this wasn't a good sign.

My mom suspected the worst. "Dave," she said to my dad, "I think Rob's relapsed."

"Why?" he asked.

"Dr. Z. wants Rob to call him about the results of yesterday's biopsy," she replied. "Dave, Rob usually has to call **him**."

"JoAnn, you're jumping to conclusions," he said. "It's probably nothing."

"Well, I hope you're right," she sighed.

I wasn't home when Dr. Z. called. After working eight hours at the agency, I stopped off at the rec center and hadn't eaten dinner yet. Since I arrived home late that evening, my mom delayed telling me about the phone call until the next day. When I came through the door, I could tell something was different in the way she asked, "So, how was your day today?" I didn't give it much thought, however, until after I called Dr. Z. the next morning.

"Rob, I'm not going to beat around the bush," Dr. Z. said. "We found some leukemia cells in your bone marrow. I'm very sorry, but as I've said many times before, this was a possibility."

My heart sank, but I wasn't surprised. My mind flashed back to the previous day. An hour before I left work, I was sitting in the medical files room, perusing over some case notes on one of my clients. Suddenly, a rush of lightheadedness hit me. For a moment, I felt like I was out at sea, floating on a raft. *It's probably nothing,* I told myself as I went about my business. Deep down, I suspected it might be more, but I put it out of my mind.

"How far has it progressed?" I asked.

"Actually, it's progressed pretty far," he replied. "After you left our clinic the other day, the pathologists studying your blood noticed some blast cells in your bloodstream. They alerted us that afternoon, and we evaluated your marrow the first chance we had."

"How are my platelets?"

"Well, they're pretty low," he said. "I believe they were 36,000."

After he told me to report to the hospital, I hung up the phone sick to my heart. I told my mom and she said, "Well, I suspected it. Listen, Rob. This is only a setback. I still believe you'll be healed."

With the return of the leukemia came feelings of sadness, anger, and disappointment. It seemed as if all of the effort I'd put into getting my life back on course had been to no avail. Instead of crying or losing my temper, I just went numb.

"Rob, scream, yell, or cry if you want to," my mom said. "Whatever you're feeling, God understands. Just don't hold it all in."

Ignoring her advice, I shook my head, sighed, and prepared for the dreaded return to the hospital. Too cool to show my emotions, I refused to go into a histrionic frenzy. While my mom phoned my dad to tell him the news, I wrote a check to Discover Card and balanced my checkbook. It had been just five minutes since my phone conversation with Dr. Z., and I'd already set my sights on regaining control.

After one relapse with AML, there's little hope for a cure outside of a BMT. Teary-eyed and apprehensive over the trials ahead, my mom stood her ground and repeated her conviction that I would be healed all the way to the hospital.

I didn't know what to say.

Perhaps, I've been fooling myself. Maybe this will never end.

My arrival on the oncology floor was a "kick in the teeth." The same nurses I visited weeks earlier looked at me, and their faces fell. One stopped dead in her tracks and asked, "Why are you here?" Now my pride, as well as my faith, had taken a blow.

Just 11 months earlier, Dr. Z. had come into my room and announced that my leukemia had gone into remission. Since then, I'd reasserted the same cockiness about my health and stamina that characterized my life before the diagnosis. It was subtle, but deep down, I considered myself the "star patient" at Georgetown; the plumb line by which all other cancer patients should be compared. Instead of thanking God every day for how far he'd brought me, I'd fallen into the same routine of taking my health for granted.

My mom later told me she noticed this shift in my attitude a month earlier while I was working in the front yard. Our mulcher had become clogged, and as I was cleaning it out, she walked over to me and said, "I don't think it's good for you to be breathing all that stuff. You need to put on a mask."

"I don't need one. I'm fine," I replied.

"Rob, you just went through chemotherapy seven months ago," she said. "Using that thing without a mask isn't good for anyone, and your resistance is still low."

"Mom, my lungs are great. Don't worry about it!" I said, becoming irritated.

"Well, you do what you want," she huffed. "But I think you should wear a mask. I would if I were you."

"Well, you're not me!" I said flatly. "I can handle it, so stop nagging me!"

My mom said that as she walked away, she thought to herself, *I won't be surprised if he relapses because he hasn't learned a thing from last year.*

Dr. Z. met with me and my parents in the oncology floor waiting room to discuss my status. "Since AML is so aggressive, we have little time to waste in our search for a donor," he said. "Our plan now is to change your status to 'urgent' and start you on Re-induction Therapy to induce a second remission while we wait for the donor to be located."

"How long will it last?" I asked.

"It will be similar to the same treatment you had last year," he replied. "In addition to seven days of Ara-C, we'll be using *VP-16* and *Daunarubicin.* We're adding VP-16, because it's often effective with relapsed patients such as yourself, and it won't increase the overall toxicity to your system."

During the course of our discussion, he told my parents, "We all think very highly of Robert, and we want to make sure we provide him with the best care possible."

"Thank you," my mom said.

"Now, Rob, I know you probably don't want to hear any more bad news today, but we'll need to do another biopsy today so we can run specialized tests to determine whether we're dealing with the same strain of AML as last year or something different," he said.

"That's okay,' I assured him. "It's not anything I haven't been through before."

My return to Georgetown began as a virtual repeat of the previous summer. A new Hickman catheter was surgically implanted the next day, and Dr. L., the intern who monitored my care in the waning days of June '92, was now completing her first year of residency. As I passed the nurses' desk, she recognized me and said, "There's Mr. Brown!"

"Hey, how are you?" I asked.

"I'm doing well," she said. "And yourself?"

I relapsed," I said, smiling weakly.

"I know," she said. "I just heard. I'll drop by later to check up on you."

I always liked her, even though I was only under her care a few days. Like Dr. M., the intern in charge of my care in July '92, she treated me like a person and took time to chat with me as she drew my blood or checked my vital signs. During the course of my treatments, I saw her a few times while walking the halls of the hospital, and she always had a kind word. A Christian herself, she told me the previous summer that she'd be praying for me after she moved to another floor. That meant a lot.

This summer I needed her prayers even more. I threw up several times that first weekend, and when I went for a walk that Sunday afternoon, my IV line got snagged in a doorway, pulling my new catheter out so it no longer worked. The next day, my catheter was removed, and I received the remaining four days of my chemo via peripheral IVs.

Some of my closest friends visited me, and several others called or sent a card the moment they heard of my relapse. However, no onslaught of visitors or greeting cards descended upon me like the previous July. I suspected, and these suspicions were later borne out, that less people visited or sent regards because many of them didn't know what to say now that my leukemia had returned. What **do** you say to someone who has relapsed after spending the past year telling everyone God has cured him? That's a hard question. I can't speak for everyone, but I just wanted people to treat me like they did before the relapse. I didn't want their pity.

Unlike July '92, I had the energy to do more than just lay around on my bed and shoot the breeze. When I received visitors, I often took them up to the sixth floor balcony so we could go outside and escape my stuffy hospital room. I wanted my friends to see me as they've always known me, not as a sick, weakened cancer patient on his last gasp of life. I worried that their faith might be shaken or that they might feel sorry for me. I wanted them to know, more than anything else, that my present state of affairs was a set-back, not my final call. Most important, I refused to allow them to see the side of me which was angry at God and fearful of what may transpire in the next several months. Over and over again, I told my friends and family (and to some extent, myself), "It's only temporary. Don't worry about a thing."

The most striking event which happened that week involved my roommate. A man in his early to mid-60s, his looks and personality reminded me of my Uncle Joe. He was kind and personable; a family man and a golfer. When I asked him why he was there, he explained that he had been treated for cancer earlier in the year and now experienced ungodly back pain from all his surgeries. He seemed fairly healthy after all he'd been through, but the next day, he was writhing in pain.

"Ooohh! It's unbearable . . . someone make it stop!" he cried out in agony as his wife and family kept watch beside his bed.

I listened to him moan and groan for hours. I felt awful, not only because I knew he was suffering, but also because I just wanted him to shut up so I could get some sleep.

Why won't someone give him some Morphine or something?

Later that afternoon, I learned the awful truth when his doctor reported the results of his latest CAT scan: the cancer had returned and metastasized to the extent that nothing could be done. This information was confidential, but a thin curtain was all that divided my side of the room from his. I heard everything.

Upon hearing the news, my roommate broke down and cried. This is the first time I've ever witnessed a grown man cry with such a lack of inhibition. I felt sorry for him and his family.

"That's all right," the doctor said. "What you're doing is appropriate. Just let it out."

More crying.

Several minutes passed. I can't remember much of what was said after that, but before he left, the doctor assured him that although they couldn't treat his cancer, they could manage his pain and make the final months of his life more comfortable. "We'll implant a catheter into your spine so you can receive narcotics to manage your pain and enable you to enjoy the time you have remaining with your family," he said.

The only thing my roommate could do when the doctor had finished was ask if he would be able to play golf, to which the doctor answered in the affirmative.

I knew several patients who had died since my diagnosis the previous summer. Every time I went for a walk around the hospital, I passed the rooms of terminally ill patients. Death had been all around me, but because I was so focused on my own recovery, I blocked it all out of my mind. When my roommate was told his condition was terminal, however, death by cancer became real and personal. I knew that unless God intervened, I would be in his shoes a few months later.

Before I relapsed, I knew God might not heal me according to my time schedule, but I refused to think about it. Over time, I convinced myself that I was already healed. Now I wondered if I'd been self-deceived from the very beginning.

Maybe God never spoke to me in the ER last year, and I made the whole thing up to cope with the horror of my present circumstances. Perhaps the peace I felt was just a flight to fantasy. How can I be so sure Ruth and Dad's "words of knowledge" weren't just wishful thinking? I've studied enough theology to know they don't carry the authority of Scripture itself.

These doubts swirled in my mind for days, but I couldn't ignore how God had worked in my life the previous year. From my perspective, I had a long way to go before I fulfilled my calling.

Perhaps the relapse is part of God's grand design. Maybe there's a purpose here that goes far beyond what I've always believed to be God's will for my life.

I have to give my roommate credit for asking if he'd still be able to play golf. In spite of what he'd just learned about his future, he still wanted to get everything he could out of the time he had left. Over the past year, I had met a number of cancer patients who looked at life through his eyes. They weren't ashamed to express their fears and sadness, and they tried to live each day to the fullest

because they had no guarantees. I sometimes echoed similar senti-
ments, but truth be known, I was never a good existentialist. I tend
to think too much in terms of what the future may bring, not what
today already holds.

Knowing a BMT with an unrelated donor might be hell on earth,
I wasn't looking to prolong my life for a few years. I wanted nothing less than a cure. Outside of my relationship with God, nothing
meant more to me than the hope of living long enough to fulfill my
dreams of getting married, raising a family, and having a career.

CHAPTER XIV

The Heart of the Storm

Saturday, June 19, I was discharged. After seven days of chemotherapy, the only meals I tolerated were classic "American" staples like hamburgers, steak, chicken, and scrambled eggs. Anything spicy like Mexican or Chinese food tasted like tin foil and sweets just turned my stomach. I couldn't even look at a chocolate chip cookie without feeling the urge to upchuck.

As with my previous treatments, my immune system and blood levels were depleted, making me vulnerable to infections, anemia, and bleeding. Twenty-four hours after my discharge, small, purplish blotches called *petechiae* appeared on my arms and legs. A sure sign that I needed platelets, I paged Dr. B., the oncology resident on-call. Although I was going to see Dr. Z. the next morning, Dr. B. told me to return to the hospital immediately because I was in danger of internal hemorrhaging. Because outpatient transfusion services were unavailable on Sundays, I checked into the ER to avoid being admitted as an inpatient. By the time my parents and I returned home, it was past 2:00 A.M.

Spending half the night in a crowded ER and trying to get by on four hours of sleep took its toll. During the drive to the hospital to see Dr. Z. the next day, I vomited all over the front seat. The anger I'd held in since I first heard of my relapse exploded like a time bomb. "They couldn't even keep me in remission for 10 months!" I shouted, as I slammed the dashboard with my fist and let out an expletive I won't repeat. I was angry at the medical establishment for not developing a quick and painless cure for my disease, the ER staff for not attending to my needs immediately the previous night, my insurance company for refusing to cover any home infusions until August, and God for allowing this whole thing to happen in the first place. The release of that anger was well over-due. I was sick and tired of being "the compliant cancer patient whose bravery extends beyond his years."

If you're like me, it's difficult to admit anger, especially if the object of your anger is God. Some people would rather walk across fiery coals than admit they're angry with God. After all, *"Christians are never supposed to get angry with God."* It's out-of-bounds, irreverent, arrogant. The height of distrust in the Creator, it's the clay answering back to the potter in its most basic form. That said, God understands.

I'm not advocating that we ever have the right to be angry with God, but if we're honest with ourselves, most of us experience it at some point in our lives. God isn't shocked when we become angry with him because he knows our tolerance level better than we do. The times I've been the most angry at God have often foreshadowed periods of great spiritual and emotional growth. In these times, my weaknesses, insecurities, and helplessness become all the more apparent. When I finally come to my senses, all I'm left with is the admission that I have nowhere else to go but toward him. Now, back to my story . . .

Six days after my discharge from the hospital, I spiked a fever and returned to Georgetown. My fever broke the next day, but I remained in the hospital for two weeks of IV antibiotics. When my blood cultures came back negative several days after I was admitted, Dr. S., the attending physician on-call, quipped that I probably could have taken some Tylenol and stayed out of the hospital. Because I was so immune-compromised, however, we both knew that would have been unwise.

One evening, the nurse in charge of my care was someone from the BMT unit.

"Are you a new nurse here?" I asked.

"No, I'm with Bone Marrow Transplant down on 2-East," she

replied in a heavy southern accent. "They're short-staffed here on 4-BLES tonight, so I'm filling in. My name is Bonnie."

"Really? I'm supposed to undergo an unrelated BMT for leukemia sometime this fall."

"Is that right?" she asked.

"Yes. What's it like for most bone marrow patients?" I asked.

With that, she gave me an overview of what to experience. "Before you undergo an unrelated BMT, you'll have to undergo four days of total body irradiation [TBI] and three days of chemo to destroy your own marrow," she said. "After two days of rest, your new marrow will be infused into your bloodstream just as if it were another blood transfusion. It takes anywhere from 14-28 days for the marrow to engraft, and the average stay in the hospital is five to eight weeks."

"Now, am I going to be totally isolated for that whole time?" I asked.

"Only until your new marrow engrafts and begins to reproduce its own cells," she said.

"And the chemo is going to be ultra-high-dose, right?" I asked.

"Oh, believe me, you're going to be receiving the 'industrial strength' kind of stuff," she replied. "We need to make sure we destroy your old marrow so that your body can accept your donor's marrow without any complications.

"Besides hair loss, nausea and vomiting, you'll probably have severe mouth sores and throat pain caused by temporary damage to the mucous lining on the roof of your mouth and upper GI tract," she continued.

"That sounds awful," I said.

"It is," she said. "Have you ever had any problems like that before?"

"No," I replied. "I had a little bit of throat pain when I went through my second round of chemo last August, but it only lasted a couple of days."

"Well, you **will** have a problem with it this time," she said. "Most of our patients need to be fed intravenously until they can tolerate solid food again. There have been some exceptions though. Three years ago, a young woman diagnosed with Aplastic Anemia ate like a horse the entire time she was in isolation, and she went home 17 days after her transplant."

"How's she doing now?" I asked.

"She's doing great as far as I know," she replied.

"What about Graft vs. Host Disease [GVHD]?" I asked.[1]

"GVHD occurs in half of the patients who receive allogeneic BMTs," she said. "Since your donor's marrow comprises a different immune system from your own, it's cells are likely to attack anything they recognize as unfamiliar, including you."

"What if I get it?" I asked.

"It occurs in two forms, Acute and Chronic," she said. "The acute phase occurs right after engraftment and usually affects the liver, skin, and intestines. Although we can control it with immunosuppressant medications, it's still likely to cause skin rash, nausea, jaundice, and diarrhea."

"Sounds pretty rough," I surmised.

"I won't lie to you," she said. "Some of our patients with GVHD put out an average of three liters of diarrhea per day.

"Chronic GVHD doesn't arise until a few months post-transplant, but it can be a complication lasting for several years," she explained. "It's primary symptoms are skin rash, 'dry eyes,' and liver problems."

"I've heard that GVHD could keep me from relapsing again," I said.

"That's what we call the 'Graft vs. Leukemia Effect,'" she said, nodding. "Patients who experience GVHD often do better because their new immune system is more likely to recognize and destroy cancer cells that may have survived the TBI and chemotherapy. So it's definitely a blessing in disguise."

As we continued talking, she assured me that Georgetown was a wise choice for a patient facing a BMT. She had recently worked as a BMT nurse at another well-known hospital, and she said, "If I were a patient, I'd rather be here."

Our conversation was very reaffirming, and I went to sleep that night confident we were making the right choice in sticking with

---

[1] Graft vs. Host Disease (GVHD) is organ rejection in reverse. Although the liver, skin, and intestines are the most common organs affected, GVHD has been known to affect the blood cells, the heart, lungs, joints, and connective tissues. *The Signet Mosby Encyclopedia*, Rev. ed., 355.

Georgetown. Not only did they have a competent staff, but I could remain in the area with friends and family. Our family had done an extensive search on other BMT treatment centers on the east coast, and Georgetown was rated as one of the best.

Later that same week, Chris, the Counseling Director at CFC, came by to visit me along with Kelley, the Singles' Pastor. During their visit, Chris asked, "Rob, I've heard you and your parents say many times that you're convinced that it's God's will to heal you. Not that I don't believe it, but what if it turns out that you're wrong?"

"Well," I began, "God has done too many things this past year that have confirmed to me that it's his will to heal me. He never promised that I wouldn't relapse and have to go through a BMT. Of course, I was upset about that."

"I would be too," he said.

"If God calls me home early, I guess it won't really matter anymore," I added. "I know Heaven's a better place than Earth. But there's still a lot that I want to experience in this life. I want to have a career, get married, have a family, and reach people for Christ. I want to have a full life here before I die."

"So do we all!" he said, laughing. "What about your parents? How would they react if you died?"

"Well, they both believe I'll be healed. My mom's said things like, 'Rob, I firmly believe God is going to heal you. I would just about stake my life on it. After all he's done for you this past year, I would be extremely confused if he took you from us.'

"So yeah," I continued, "they'd take it hard. But I think they would eventually accept it and remain faithful to God."

"Rob," Kelley chimed in, "Over the past year, many people in the singles' ministry saw you as an example of God's healing power. Now some of them are wavering in their faith and questioning God's goodness as a result of your relapse.

"Would you be willing to talk with them about this issue when your treatments are over?" he asked. "I believe it could really help them deal with things in their own lives."

"Yes, but not right now," I replied. "When I returned to Sunday School last year you asked me to give a testimony about what God was doing in my life. I'd rather you not ask me to do so when I return this time because I'm still dealing with some of the same issues they are. I'd feel like a fraud."

"Sure," Kelley said. "Rob, the one thing they're looking for is genuineness. After your transplant though, I would like to give you and some of the other singles who have had cancer, like Kris and Randolph, the opportunity to share your experiences in an open forum where you field questions from the group. I think it could be a powerful ministry opportunity."

"I'd love to," I said.

After we made some small talk over Roy Rogers fried chicken, Chris and Kelley left and I tuned in to the Wimbleton tournament on TV. An hour later, I met with Dr. R., one of the attending physicians associated with the Department of Bone Marrow Transplantation. We hit it off well, and she seemed to take a genuine interest in me as a person. Because I'd already had an extensive conversation with a seasoned BMT nurse, I didn't ask her many questions, except one that is probably typical of a first-year medical student: "In theory, I will be receiving enough radiation and chemo to destroy my marrow," I said. "Being that leukemia begins in the marrow, why do some people who receive BMTs still relapse?"

"Robert, if you could answer that for us, you'd receive the Nobel prize in microbiology," she said. "But remember . . . it only takes one cell to cause a relapse."

"And that's why I need some GVHD," I interjected.

"Correct," she replied.

A few days after my meeting with Dr. R., I finally went home. It was already mid-July, and my white cell counts were still quite low. Since I couldn't have a biopsy until my counts were normal, I had no idea if I were back in remission. I was home four days before I returned for my biopsy, and because it was Friday afternoon, Dr. Z. told me the results wouldn't be available until Monday or Tuesday.

"Rob, from what I saw in your blood results today, I don't think we'll find a problem with your marrow," he assured me.

"Is it okay for me to attend a pool party tomorrow and church this Sunday?" I asked.

"Paint the town red," he said.

CHAPTER XV

Finding a Silver Lining

The weekend after my biopsy, I attended two pool parties, visited my friend Heather, who had just graduated from the University of Virginia, and even saw my Aunt Juanita and Uncle Butch, both of whom came up from North Carolina. Despite my bald head, I almost forgot about my illness. I hammed it up with my jokes, romped around on the sand during an outdoor volleyball game, and did all I could to show everyone I was still me. Unfortunately, my furlough from the hospital was short-lived, and I returned to the hospital on Tuesday afternoon for a second round of chemotherapy.

Although my bone marrow biopsy had confirmed a second remission, Dr. Z insisted that I undergo a six-day round of high-dose Ara-C to insure that I remained leukemia-free until the donor search was completed. I was scheduled to receive my replacement catheter on the day after my first session of chemotherapy, but due to a heavy backlog of patients, my surgery time kept getting delayed. Since I couldn't eat anything for eight hours prior to surgery, I went an entire day on chemotherapy without food. When I was finally called down to surgery the next morning, I felt absolutely lousy.

Because my second round of chemotherapy came on the heels of my Re-induction treatment in June, my immune system remained non-existent for the next three weeks. Sunday, August 1, I contracted an infection that proved to be so resistant that even three days of IV antibiotics couldn't bring down my fever. Suspecting the possibility of a fungal infection, my doctors added the dreaded Amphoteracin B to my daily cycle of medications. Legendary for its side-effects of nausea, fever, chills, and headache, Amphoteracin B can be more intolerable than chemotherapy itself. Because fungal infections often don't show up in the blood until it's too late to treat them, I remained on the drug five days even though my blood cultures initially tested negative for fungus. By the following weekend, I was so sick that I actually chose to remain in the hospital when given the option of continuing IV therapy at home.[1]

During this period, my parents and I finally met Dr. M., the director of the Georgetown BMT program. Although we were originally scheduled to meet with him at the BMT outpatient clinic, we met in my hospital room because I was still an inpatient. After exchanging pleasantries, he explained the BMT procedure and answered our questions regarding its risks and benefits, my chances for long-term survival, and the status of our search for a donor. "The preliminary results of the donor search show there are several potential matches on the national and international registries," he reported. "We're looking at two good prospects from England right now."

"How long do you think it will take before a good match is confirmed?" my dad asked.

"It's hard to judge that," Dr. M. replied. "Since there are so many variables that determine the success of marrow engraftment, such as DNA, blood type, and the sex of the donor, more sensitive tests still need to be done. It could be several more weeks at least."

"Will my own marrow be harvested as an insurance policy?" I asked.

"Yes," he said. "We'll still need to harvest some of your own bone marrow so that if your donor's marrow fails to engraft and produce its own cells, we can still do an autologous BMT."

"Okay," I said.

"If we do find a donor," he continued, "you'll need to undergo four days of TBI and three days of chemotherapy."

---

[1] My health coverage through Blue Cross/Blue Shield of VA was finally activated on August 1, 1993.

"Will I become sterile?" I asked.

"Most people receiving TBI do become sterile," he admitted.

"That's what I thought," I said.

"Have you looked into visiting a sperm bank?" he asked.

"I went last year, but I chose not to go through with it," I replied. "I assumed I could always return, but since then, I've gone through four more rounds of chemo. It's possible I'm already sterile, but even if I'm not, I'm afraid my sperm might be defective."

"That's a possibility," he said. "We don't have any ways of determining whether your donated sperm would be healthy."

"Rob, you can always adopt," my dad said.

"I know," I replied.

"Other potential risks are lung problems, cataracts, and secondary cancers later in life," Dr. M. continued. "We'll try to protect your lungs by shielding them from the radiation with custom-fitted lead plates."

"So how long will I be in the hospital?" I asked.

"After you're admitted to the BMT Unit, you'll be isolated in a Laminar Air Flow [LAF] room until the engraftment of your new marrow," he said. "Our chief concerns for you at this time will be susceptibility to bleeding and infections. For this reason, you'll receive blood and platelet transfusions until your new marrow can produce them on its own."

"What are my chances of a cure?" I asked.

"We're confident we'll cure your leukemia," he said. "However, due to the risks of infection and damage to your vital organs, there's a 10 percent chance you won't make it out of the hospital. Another problem is GVHD, but we can usually control it with steroids and IV medications such as *Cyclosporine*."

The four of us chatted a little while longer and then said our goodbyes. Meeting Dr. M. confirmed that staying with Georgetown was the right decision. We were impressed with his expertise in the field, and we saw that he had a caring, conscientious, and personable manner similar to what we had witnessed in Dr. Z. When I was finally discharged from the hospital a few days later, a silver lining appeared in the clouds that had gathered over me the past two months. I knew I would be in good hands when I embarked on the journey of my life that fall.

CHAPTER XVI

Preparing for the Road Ahead

===

A week after my discharge from the hospital, I returned in the early morning of August 25 for my bone marrow harvest. The average person undergoing a bone marrow harvest can expect a few days of mild discomfort in the hip. Because my platelets were so low, however, my backside was black and blue for two weeks. That evening, I could barely crawl in and out of bed on my own. When my friends John and Linda visited me the next day, John joked that I walked like I had rickets.

The night following my surgery, I stayed on the Bone Marrow/ Renal Transplant Unit and received a taste of what to expect later that fall. I walked past the unit once before during one of my many excursions through the hospital, but I never visited it. Frankly, I had no desire to do so because the images it conjured up of complete isolation from the world unnerved me. Closed off to the rest of the floor by design, it could only be entered through two sets of automatic doors. It had its own hepa-filtered air system to reduce the spread of airborne infections, and contained a sign warning visitors of the dangers they posed to those inside:

OCCUPANTS HAVE EXTREMELY DIMINISHED IMMUNE SYSTEMS AND ARE SUSCEPTIBLE TO OUTSIDE INFECTIONS

It was definitely not a Holiday Inn.

My LAF room was the size of a regular hospital room, but it was divided in half by a plastic curtain which itself was enclosed by a metal frame door that could swing open or closed. Devoid of a bathroom or sink to minimize the spread of bacteria, the patient living area consisted of a bed, miniature bureau, TV, exercise bike, and portable toilet. The front half of the room contained a wash basin near the door, but it was to be used by medical personnel only.

The windows were extra-thick and double-walled to prevent the infiltration of outdoor pollutants, and the LAF fans, which were located in the wall behind my bed, provided a steady, unidirectional flow of sterile air that was so dry it made my eyes sting. The low, whirring sound of these fans caused the whole room to vibrate and reminded me of boarding a 747. The controls to the LAF fans, lights, window shades, TV, and "privacy curtain" were right at my bedside. In another setting, the room could have passed for one of Tim Allen's creations on *Home Improvement.*

Following my discharge from the hospital the next afternoon, I spent two months at home. During that time, my parents and I kept the road to Georgetown hot. In addition to routine visits with Dr. Z. and multiple consultations with Bone Marrow Transplantation and Radiation Medicine, I underwent a pre-BMT screening that included an EKG, CAT scan of the chest, abdomen, and pelvis, 24-hour urine analysis, and a host of other tests assessing whether or not I was a good candidate for a BMT.

Many patients who can tolerate standard chemotherapy are poor candidates for BMTs because of their assault on the immune system, internal organs, and psyche. Whereas standard chemotherapy attempts to kill the cancer cells without harming the marrow, an allogeneic BMT is a process by which the diseased marrow is **destroyed** and replaced by the marrow of a donor. The procedure is so radical that its risks sometimes outweigh its benefits. These risks include an increased susceptibility to infections residing inside the body as well those invading from the outside, and the possibilities of graft failure, GVHD, and damage to vital organs.

Due to my youth and good baseline health, my odds of surviving were good, provided that a donor were located. However, the odds of finding a suitable donor, even for Anglo-Saxons like myself, are one in 20,000. With ethnic minorities or persons with a mixed-racial background, finding a donor is even more difficult. All I could do was wait and pray.

In mid-September, my miracle came true when a suitable donor was found in England. I can only attribute my good fortune to the grace of God. When I announced the news to my Sunday School class the following week, the whole room erupted in cheers. To celebrate the occasion, my friend April, a member of the class, treated me to dinner at Outback Steakhouse.

After my donor was located and my BMT was scheduled for mid-October, I did everything I could to increase my chances for surviving the procedure. My recent chemotherapy treatments had reduced me to a shell of my former self. If it weren't for my good health at the time of my relapse, things would have been even worse.

Getting back into reasonable shape became a top priority. Exercising helped relieve the pent-up stress of the past three months and allowed me to forget I was a cancer patient. I never fully regained the strength I enjoyed months earlier, but I was romping on the stair machine and pumping iron as if I were a normal person within a matter of weeks. If it hadn't been for my catheter, which restricted me from engaging in heavy lifting or rigorous sports, there would have been nothing I wouldn't have done.

Knowing I was going to be in isolation after I was admitted for my BMT, my social life became a priority as well. I went out with friends whenever I could, resumed my involvement at church, attended two weddings, and made plans to go on a three-day weekend retreat with my Singles' group to Virginia Beach.

My friends were indispensable. They didn't fully understand what I was going through, but like me, they had experienced pain at some point in their lives. One of the first persons to visit me in the hospital that past summer was my friend Christina, who had lost her mother to a long fight with breast cancer the previous April. Still in emotional turmoil and reluctant to even walk through the doors of a hospital, she visited me and offered me encouragement just days after my relapse. When I talked with her two months later at a wedding she and I attended, she said that visiting me had been a major step in helping her to move on with her life.

Friends like Christina couldn't explain why God had allowed something bad to happen to me no more than I could make sense of why cancer took her mom from her. But that didn't matter. They were there for me when I needed them, not only to pray for me, but also to offer their support and treat me as if I were still a regular person. I wanted to be seen as **Rob**, not a cancer patient. I am sure it was a struggle, especially before my hair and mustache started growing back, but they honored my wishes without my even asking them.

As for my relationship with God, it was another story. He should have been at the forefront of my mind, but my social life and drive to regain a sense of control became so important that my priorities got out of line. My daily time in prayer and the Word became an afterthought. Sure, I was angry that God had allowed me to relapse, and more than likely, that contributed to my spiritual malaise. But I was also so focused on surviving that I didn't even want to spend time trying to sort through all my feelings about God's justice and will for my life. I just wanted to get the BMT over and done with, so I could focus on my own agenda.

My mom confronted me one evening about my spiritual life. I hemmed and hawed about it, and she asked, "Do you think you're just going to waltz right into your BMT with no preparation whatsoever?"

I had no answer for her. I knew she was talking about the preparation of my heart. When a soldier enters into combat, he must have more going for him than being in good shape and knowing how to fire a rifle. The intangibles of a good soldier, such as character, bravery, trust in one's comrades, and singleness of mind aren't developed overnight. The difference between me and an infantryman was the nature of the war. The BMT ahead was a fight for my life against leukemia, infections, treatments with dreadful side-effects, and isolation from the world.

CHAPTER XVII

Submitting to the Potter

A week before I returned to the hospital for my BMT, I joined my singles' group for a retreat to Virginia Beach, VA. I hadn't been to the ocean in two years, and I couldn't have asked for better weather. Running and frolicking on the beach, tossing the frisbee, and breathing in the fresh, salty air was the best thing I could do for myself before I returned to Georgetown. Strangely enough, I almost didn't go. Just two days earlier, my sinuses became so congested that I cancelled out on the retreat, fearing my transplant might be delayed if I had a sinus infection.

Friday morning, when the group was preparing to leave for the beach, I went in for an appointment with Dr. C., the BMT outpatient physician. I told him of my decision to stay home from the retreat, and he looked at me with a surprised, almost disgusted look.

"Why did you go and do that for?" he asked.

"Well, I don't want to be battling a sinus infection when I go in for my BMT," I said.

"That's no reason to stay home from the beach," he countered. "You need a vacation. The beach is the best place to go if you're having problems with your sinuses."

"So, you don't think it's a problem if I go, provided I'm careful and take an antibiotic or antihistamine?" I asked.

"Sure, go right ahead. Enjoy yourself," he replied.

"Well, I need to call my friend April," I said. "She and I were going to ride down together. Hopefully she hasn't left yet."

"By all means, use my phone," Dr. C. said.

When I called April, she told me a space had just become available because my friend Larry had called in sick. Because his spot was already paid for, I went for free!

God obviously wanted me to go on that retreat. Pastor Kelley, who had recently accepted a call to be the Singles Minister at a church in Michigan, would be leaving his post as our Singles' Minister the very day I was scheduled to enter the hospital. For the past year, I had sat under his ministry and been challenged to live as a dedicated follower of Christ. This was going to be the last time I'd hear him teach, and he couldn't have chosen a more timely topic. The theme for that weekend, *Who is the potter? Who is the clay?*, revolved around the following Scriptures and hit me square in the eyes:

> "You turn things upside down, as if the potter were thought to be like the clay! Shall what is formed say to him who formed it, 'He did not make me?' Can the pot say of the potter, 'He knows nothing?' "[1]

> "Yet, O Lord, you are our Father. We are the clay, you are the potter; we are all the work of your hand."[2]

I had one week left until I returned for my BMT, and I was still answering back to God as a pot would to its potter. It wasn't as if I were burning with hatred toward him because I had a life-threatening illness. Time and time again over the past four months, I had reaffirmed the promise I made to him a year earlier when I said I was willing to learn whatever he wanted to teach me through my illness. That said, I didn't want to go through a BMT, and I resented him for allowing my life to be disrupted just at the time it seemed to be going somewhere.

I'm amazed at how much I had in common with Naaman, the

---

[1] Isaiah 29:16
[2] Isaiah 64:8
[3] II Kings Chapter 5

Aramean military commander whom Elisha healed of leprosy.[3] When he came to the prophet to receive a healing touch from God, Elisha told him to bathe in the Jordan River seven times. His reaction was identical to mine when I relapsed.

> "But Naaman went away angry and said, 'I thought that he would surely come out to me and stand and call on the name of the LORD his God, wave his hand over the spot and cure me of my leprosy. Are not Abana and Pharpar, the rivers of Damascus, better than any of the waters of Israel? Couldn't I wash in them and be cleansed?' So he turned and went off in a rage."[4]

Like Naaman, I enjoy living according to my own set of rules and having things go my way. If God, people or circumstances prevent that from happening, I sometimes become angry and lose sight of the fact that God knows what's best. Being a Christian doesn't make me immune to having sour grapes when my life doesn't go as planned.

The rest of Naaman's story tells us that his servant convinced him to do what Elisha said. Sure enough, Naaman was healed, and as a result, he became a devout follower of God.[5] If he had persisted in his pride or only washed **six** times, he would have never been healed and we might have never heard of him. Worse yet, God wouldn't have done an even more important work in his heart and through his life.

That weekend at Virginia Beach, God showed me that in the same way a potter molds and pounds a lump of clay to shape it into an object of worth, he was allowing this rough time in my life to strip me of my pride and transform me into someone who better reflected the image of his Son. My relapse had already forced me to acknowledge that God was more concerned with my maturity and character than whether my life progressed according to schedule. His will to heal me seemed as crystal clear now as it did 16 months earlier, but submitting to him and allowing him free reign in my life, regardless of how long that healing took, was up to me.

---

[4] II Kings 5:12
[5] II Kings 5:13-19

As I'm writing this, I'm reminded of Ephesians 2:10, which says, "For we are his workmanship, created in Christ Jesus to do good works, which God prepared in advance for us to do." Shortly after I was first diagnosed with leukemia, my former high school youth pastor, Jeff, wrote me a letter in which he quoted that scripture and said:

> I don't know if you're aware of that word "workmanship" or not. It comes from the Greek word "poeima," from which we get the word "poem." God is writing a masterpiece into your life, Rob. Each line as it is written forms a part of the whole . . . some appear to fit and some lines don't seem to rhyme at all! I've often asked, "God, what in the world is ever going to rhyme with this line you've just written?!" I imagine coming down with an illness like you have could provoke that same question. My brother, some day when we see all things from God's perspective, every line will make sense and a beautiful poem will be seen.

He's right. Our lives are poems written by the hand of God, and each line only makes sense when it's read in context. Going through a relapse made no sense in my eyes. Nevertheless, I returned to Georgetown for my BMT on October 17, 1993 confident that when God finished writing this part of my story, I would look back and see his guiding hand every step of the way.

CHAPTER XVIII

The First Leg

Sunday morning, October 17, I went to church one final time to say goodbye to the friends who had stood by me the past 16 months. Newcomers to our Sunday School class would have never guessed that I had leukemia. Decked out in a red satin tie and Perry Ellis action slacks, I sported a full head of hair and a mustache. My 187 pounds filled out my six-foot frame, and I looked and acted as if I were in the bloom of health. I was facing the most toxic treatment known to medical oncology, but I told everyone it was just the last bump in the road to recovery.

That Sunday morning was Kelley's last as the Singles' Minister at CFC. "I don't want to leave today without taking the time to pray for Rob Brown," he said as he ended the class. "As most of you know, Rob will check into Georgetown University Medical Center later this afternoon to have a bone marrow transplant that will hopefully cure his leukemia. Folks, what he's facing is no small matter. This is serious stuff.

"Rob," he continued, "come on up front so we can lay our hands on you and pray for God's healing and protection while you're in the hospital."

When the group gathered around and laid their hands on me, it was a fitting end to the past year. They had become like family to me. Outside my immediate family and close relatives, there wasn't a soul in the world that I wanted in my corner more than them. When they finished praying, I hugged Kelley and several others, reassuring them that my departure was only temporary. "I'll see you all in the Spring," I said. "Keep my seat warm."

Later that afternoon, I unpacked my belongings in the same LAF room I spent the night in two months earlier. Debbie, the nurse in charge of my care, introduced herself and explained LAF protocol. As a BMT patient in isolation, I needed to follow strict procedures of hygiene, such as gargling with sodium bicarbonate to reduce the chance of mouth sores and taking cultures of my throat, ears, nose, and rectum three times a day to rule out infections.

"When using the portable toilet," she began, "you need to line the bowl with a plastic bag to catch your stools so they can be disposed of by the nurse. We'll provide you with sterile gauzes to use as toilet paper. In order to avoid rectal infections, you need to pour some of this betadine solution onto each gauze before you use it," she said, as she demonstrated.

"Okay," I said.

"Visitors must wash their hands and wear disposable surgical masks, gowns, caps, and shoe covers," she said. "All nurses, doctors, and support staff are required to wear them as well."

These precautions sound excessive, but believe me, they're necessary. While BMT patients are in isolation, their environment must be as close to sterile as possible because the most trivial of cold viruses can be life-threatening. That said, rules for LAF protocol have actually become more relaxed in recent years.

In the early days of BMTs, no one was allowed behind the curtain, except in emergencies. Medical personnel remained on the other side and used the plastic sleeves attached to the curtain to take blood, administer medications, and check vital signs. Today, many BMT centers, Georgetown included, allow doctors, nurses, and family members behind the curtain, provided that the LAF fans are turned on high, and they're wearing the aforementioned attire.

After Debbie finished her instructions and left to attend to the needs of other patients, my parents and I said our goodbyes. It was time for dinner, and as I settled down to watch the Cardinals skunk the Redskins, I put on my game face. In just 12 hours I would be starting four days of TBI, followed by three days of heavy-duty chemotherapy (VP-16 and *Cytoxin*). I knew the accumulated toxic-ity might kill me or cause irreparable damage to my vital organs, but I'd already decided I was in this thing for the long haul. Every time I went down to the Department of Radiation Medicine for my TBI sessions, I made a declaration of faith in God's healing and protection.

Fractionated into twelve sessions to reduce the risk of severe lung disease and the side-effects of nausea and vomiting, TBI began Monday morning. During each session, I stripped down to my underwear and stood upright in a frame fitted with custom-made lead plates designed to protect my lungs. As the radiation hit my body with near-perfect precision, I remained motionless, sometimes for as long as 30 minutes. I knew the slightest shuffle could damage my lungs, but I'm fidgety by nature. Standing motionless in a semi-crouched position was one of the hardest things I've ever had to do. Telling me not to scratch made things even worse.

Unlike my previous experiences with chemotherapy, the nausea and fatigue that followed my TBI sessions were intermittent and sudden. I could be feeling fine at one moment and then, five minutes later, upchucking into a bedpan. In spite of this unpre-dictability, I tried to maintain a semblance of normalcy. I took off the hospital gown and changed back into sweats after each TBI session, resisted shaving my mustache until it became obvious it wouldn't last, and ate prepackaged, microwavable meals instead of hospital food.[1]

More stressful than how I felt was knowing I'd have to remain behind the plastic curtain for five weeks. I'm not claustrophobic, but the reality of how long I'd be confined to such a tiny living space hit me like a bombshell Monday evening. Before I was admitted, I assumed a month in the LAF room was no big deal. Now, I wondered if I could make it past a few days without losing my mind.

I've been in walk-in closets that are roomier than this! And I'm going to be in here for a month?! No walking the halls, no going downstairs to buy a cup of coffee or a newspaper whenever I feel

---

[1] Due to the threat of germs, these were only outside foods allowed on the BMT unit.

like it . . . . What did I get myself into?

The more I looked around at my cramped living space and the curtain separating me from the rest of civilization, the faster my heart pounded. For the first time in my life, I feared I might have a panic attack.

I don't know if I can keep this up without going crazy. God, I'm about ready to scream!

As I lay there obsessing over the prospect of spending the next month in a broom closet, it dawned on me that the *Sudafed* I was taking to treat my recent sinus infection might be compounding my anxiety. When I'm on a decongestant for more than a week, the most insignificant things can set me on edge. This time, it was the constant clicking of my IV machine.

I swear, I'm going to throw that thing against the wall! Why does it have to click every time it dispenses a drop of saline? The IV machines on the oncology floor don't do that. Am I going to have to put up with that for five weeks?! Because if I am, that's going to be a real problem!

I couldn't get any sleep that night until Pat, the nurse in charge of my care, came by to take my vital signs. When I told her I could only stand living in such a cramped room for so long, she stayed for a while to talk with me and put me at ease. I can't remember the content of our conversation, but it wasn't important anyhow. I needed to talk with someone who understood how I felt and had seen countless others before me experience the same thing. She assured me that if they could survive the LAF experience without going mad, I could as well.

"Is there anything else I can do for you, Rob?" she asked.

"I think I've been on Sudafed too long, and it's making me nervous," I replied. "Can my medication be changed to *Benadryl*? I've got to get some sleep tonight."

"Sure," she said, and she notified the doctor on-call about my situation. I didn't sleep well that night, but I'm convinced I wouldn't have slept at all if I'd kept everything bottled up inside. My conversation with Pat calmed my nerves so I could remind myself that my strength came from God and not my ability to adapt to my surroundings.

I finished TBI on Thursday evening, and I began my three days of chemotherapy on Friday morning. Over the weekend, two friends of mine, April and Michael, came for a visit. They were the only members of my singles' group who visited me while I was in the LAF room because shortly thereafter, I became too sick to see anyone outside of my family. I wanted to hug them, but the only thing I could do was look at them through the plastic curtain. April, who had become one of my closest friends that past year, later told me how hard it was to hold back her tears while watching me struggle to eat macaroni and cheese without vomiting.

I received my new marrow on Wednesday, Oct. 27, 1993. Harvested in England that morning and flown to Washington D.C. that night, the gift of prolonged life was hung on an IV pole and infused as if it were just another transfusion. The head pharmacist at Georgetown was the courier, and along with the marrow, he brought a miniature bottle of champagne, a get-well card signed by the flight crew, and a book covering the sights and personality of England.

Receiving my new marrow made the past few months all seem worthwhile. I assumed that I'd be out of there and on the road to recovery in just a few short weeks.

CHAPTER XIX

Trial by Fire

Two days before I received my new marrow, I ceased eating solid food. A week had passed since I began TBI, and now I couldn't even drink water without excruciating pain. My lips were chapped, the roof of my mouth and gums were covered with sores, and the mucous lining from the top of my esophagus to the bottom of my upper GI tract had become inflamed. Dr. R., the attending physician in charge of my care, told me I now had *Mucositis,* the condition Bonnie warned me about when she was my night nurse three months earlier.

"We're going to take you off solid food for now because your throat and GI tract are too sensitive," she said. "Starting this afternoon, you'll be receiving *Total Parental Nutrition [TPN]* intravenously until your GI tract heals. All of your essential vitamins and nutrients will be provided round-the-clock, so don't worry about a thing. This is normal."

"Can I still take in fluids or eat things like popsicles or ice cream?" I asked.

"Popsicles are great, but ice cream is a no-no," she replied. "Dairy products would increase the likelihood of the Mucositis becoming infected, and we don't want that. Besides, they'd make the pain worse. Popsicles, sherbet, and jello are all okay.

"It might take several weeks for your GI tract to heal," she explained. "At that time, provided you're not experiencing GHVD in your gut, we'll reintroduce you to solid food, adding one new item to the menu each day so as to not upset your digestive system. In the meantime, keep rinsing out your mouth and gums because that will help reduce your pain and the possibility of infection. I've written you prescriptions for 'magic mouthwash' to treat your mouth sores and IV pain medications to make you more comfortable. Okay?"

"Sure," I said, and she left to attend to the needs of another patient.

I felt miserable for the next three weeks. I took multiple pain medications, but they provided only temporary relief. I had so many sores in my mouth that, according to Brenda, the color of the inside of my lips was "bluish-black." My GI tract felt as if someone had dragged a fresh piece of sandpaper from the roof of my mouth to bottom of my esophagus, and I coughed up so much bloody mucous that I required a suction device to clear out my mouth and throat. I'd been warned about Mucositis, but I never thought it could be this bad. Months later, my mom told me the doctors considered my case life-threatening; an infection waiting to happen.

During my third week in the hospital, my cousin Tommy came to visit me while he was on one of his business trips. I was so strung out on pain medications that my mom had to carry the conversation. He was shaken over how much the BMT had ravaged my body. The last time he'd seen me was at our cousin Angie's wedding five months earlier when I looked as healthy as ever. Now I was bald, underweight, and barely coherent.

If Mucositis were not enough to deal with, my physicians had an even more serious problem on their hands. Severe lung problems are always a risk for BMT patients because they have no immune system to fight diseases such as Bronchitis or Pneumonia. Due to their poor prognosis, severe lung problems are one of the BMT physician's top concerns. For this reason, the radiologists take chest X-rays every morning to trouble-shoot any problems before they became unmanageable. Their fears were realized during the first week of November when my chest X-rays indicated that my lungs were filling up with fluid.

Fearing a fungal infection or Viral Pneumonia, both of which are often fatal in BMT patients, the BMT staff consulted a pulmonary specialist and the Department of Thoracic Surgery. An open lung biopsy was the best way of determining if a BMT patient has developed a secondary lung infection, but I was a poor candidate for such an invasive procedure. Because my new marrow hadn't engrafted yet, I had no immune system and no ability to manufacture blood or platelets. Therefore, it was only going to be done as a last resort.

The alternative treatment of choice was a *bronchoscopy*, a procedure in which a thin, lighted tube known as a bronchoscope was inserted into my windpipe for the purpose of viewing my bronchial tubes and withdrawing the excess contents for examination. Due to my severe mucositis, that bronchoscopy was the most unpleasant medical experience I've ever endured. I coughed, gagged, and thrashed so violently during the procedure that I had to be restrained. I felt as if I were drowning in my own mucous. Worse yet, the results were inconclusive.

I never foresaw these complications. Over the past two weeks, I'd held firm to my conviction that God would keep me safe from infection until my new marrow engrafted and my blood counts returned to normal. Now, I felt so vulnerable that I asked my dad to spend the night with me twice that week. He couldn't stay in my room, but just knowing he was in the waiting room at the end of the hallway was enough.

"Dad, I just want to thank you for spending the night with me tonight," I told him one night when he came in to check on me.

"Oh, you don't have to thank me for it Rob," he said. "I'm your father, and I would do anything for you."

"I know you would, and I want you to know that I couldn't have had a better father than you," I said. "This really means a lot."

"Well, I'm happy to do it," he replied.

"Dad, you and I have often had our disagreements in recent years, and there's been sometimes when I haven't really liked you." I said.

"Oh, there's been times when I haven't liked you either," my dad laughed.

"Yeah, but I really love and appreciate you," I explained. "When I get better, I hope our relationship will continue to improve. I look forward to the time when I can be out working with you in the yard once again. I'd like to help you take down some of those trees in the back later this spring if I'm up to it."

"Absolutely," he said. "You always do good work. I never have to worry about whether you'll do a job right."

"Well, anyway, I really appreciate your being here," I said. We talked a while longer, and I started to ramble and repeat myself, a common side-effect of being on high levels of *Dilaudid*. After he left to catch a few hours of shut-eye before he left for work, I felt a deep love for my dad that I hadn't experienced since childhood. The absurdity of the resentment I once held toward him became all the more obvious.

As the week wore on, I continued to go downhill. I was sicker now than I'd ever been during those seven days of hell in July '92. Fluid continued to build up in my lungs, and my breathing became so labored that I had to take a breath whenever I talked. The medical staff became gravely concerned. Dr. R., who usually called me "Robert" (everyone else called me "Rob"), started calling me by my childhood nickname, "Robby," by the week's end. Although she didn't want me to go through an open lung biopsy because it might sign my death warrant, she was running out of options. Everyone suspected the worst.

Even Randall, the radiologist who took my chest X-ray each morning, knew I was in trouble. A strong Christian, Randall was always cheerful and optimistic when he came into my room. Every time I saw him, he'd say, "Rob, God is going to heal you. Before you know it, you'll be on TV preaching the Gospel and telling everyone what Jesus has done in your life."

"Amen, brother," I'd say in return.

Thursday morning, November 11, he was solemn. As I stood in front of the X-ray machine, he came over, gave me a hug and said, "It's okay brother. It's alright. Just hang in there and keep your head up. Everything's going to be all right."

I don't know if he said it to convince himself or encourage me, but it didn't matter. At that time, his gesture meant the world to me.

That evening, Dr. R. came to my room while my parents were still at the hospital. My mom had been by my side all day long, and my dad had just stopped in after work. When we saw the ashen look on her face, the three of us knew she didn't have good news.

"Robby, we've been discussing your situation all afternoon," she began, "and we've concluded that our only option is an open lung biopsy. We considered a less invasive means of obtaining a biopsy that wouldn't require surgery under general anesthesia, but your platelets are too low."

'When will this procedure take place?" my mom asked.

"We're trying to schedule it for tomorrow evening," she said. "The team of thoracic surgeons handling your biopsy will come by to speak with you later this evening." Grabbing my hand, she said, "Robby, if you have a secondary lung infection, we need to find out right away. If we wait for it to show up in your blood cultures, it could be too late."

"I understand," I said.

I tried to remain confident that everything would turn out alright, but I was scared. I knew I might not survive the operation. The doctors and nurses tried their best not to show it in front of me, but I could tell they feared I might not make it. That night, I had a dream in which the spirit of River Phoenix, the young actor who died of a drug overdose shortly before I received my BMT, tried to possess my body.

When I woke up, I said, "Dad . . . that guy."

Puzzled, my father (who was spending the night with me again) asked me, "Rob, what guy are you talking about?"

Becoming more agitated, I said, "That guy!"

"Who are you talking about?" he asked.

I answered, "River Pheonix. I think he's trying to take control of my body."

This story may sound humorous, and my family and I still laugh about it. My bizarre dream could probably be attributed to the drugs I was receiving, but I think it also played out my unconscious fear of dying. I'd only seen one of River Phoenix's movies (*Sneakers*), so it wasn't as if I were a fan. However, his death impacted me because he was close to me in age. I knew that, given my precarious condition, I might join him in the grave.

I underwent the open lung biopsy on the evening of Friday, Nov. 12, my brother's 28th birthday. As I was taken down to surgery, the nurses hugged my parents and tried to comfort them, knowing it was sheer agony for them to see me taken down to surgery as if I were a lamb to the slaughter. Dr. R. called a half-hour nurses' meeting after I left to explain the reasoning behind my surgery because many of them protested. They had good reason to be concerned. Several BMT patients had died of the procedure in the past, many of whom were in better condition than me. The surgeon who conducted the operation told my parents, "I won't lie to you. What he's about to go through is extremely dangerous."

Although everything looked negative on the surface, God gave us a sign to show he was still in control. On the evening of Nov. 11, my blood results indicated that my white cells had begun to return. It had only been two weeks since I received my marrow, but it looked as if it had already started to engraft. When my parents told Dr. R., she discounted my white count as a computer glitch. Moments before I left for surgery the following afternoon, however, we received word that my white cell count had **doubled** over night. My mom says that when she heard the news, she took it as a sign that I'd survive the procedure.

A few hours before my surgery, April's parents, Carl and Bonnie, came to the hospital to spend time with my parents and pray for my safety. Neither of them knew my parents, but none of that mattered. They said God told them to go to the hospital to pray with and offer their support to my parents. To this day, my parents are grateful for the love shown by these two virtual strangers.

The open lung biopsy went by without a hitch. While I was under general anesthesia, a chest tube was inserted into my left side to drain the excess fluid from my lungs, and a small piece of my left lung was removed for analysis. I have no recollection of the events immediately following the procedure, but my parents report that I woke up so agitated that Dr. R. had to bring them into the recovery room to calm me down.

"When I first saw you," my mom later told me, "your face was swollen and tubes were coming out of you from everywhere. As you were lying there so frightened and fragile, you looked completely helpless."

As bad as I looked, I tolerated the procedure so well I was taken back to my LAF room instead of the ICU. Pat, who had been a member of the BMT nursing staff for years, said I was the only patient she knew who returned to the BMT floor immediately following an open lung biopsy. Later that night, I woke up so disoriented that my first instinct was to pull the oxygen tube out of my nose and push my nurse away every time she tried to replace it. We went back and forth several times before I finally relented.

Confined to my bed for several days because of the large chest tube in my side, I remained on oxygen for a week. Two days after the surgery, Dr. M, the BMT department head, came by and reported, "The biopsy results came back negative."

"That's great!" my mom said.

"It is," Dr. M. agreed. "After your lungs are clear, we'll remove the chest tube."

I breathed a sigh of relief at hearing the news. In retrospect, scrapping the open lung biopsy and inserting a chest tube in my side to pump out the fluid would have been sufficient. However, given my clinical picture days earlier, I would have done the same thing had I been in my doctors' shoes.

During the week following my surgery, the surgeons removed the chest tube and a bone marrow biopsy indicated that my marrow had engrafted. Pleased with my progress, the BMT staff transferred me to a regular hospital room next door. After five weeks of hell on earth, a rapid recovery seemed imminent.

CHAPTER XX

Alive, But Not Kicking

Despite the improvement in my status, I felt as if my insides had been churned in a blender. I took antinausea medications and antacids round-the-clock, but they did little to soothe my tweaked GI system. Several times, I vomited a bright, greenish liquid the nurses told me was pure stomach acid. Mucositis continued to be a problem, and I suffered nose bleeds for weeks. Outside of popsicles and sherbet, ingesting the softest of foods was torture. My most enduring memory of my first weekend out of the LAF room was struggling for a half-hour to down an eight-ounce cup of jello. It was like trying to eat steak with strep throat.

Acute GVHD compounded my problems. Thanks to the TBI, my skin already looked as if I'd been to the desert without sunscreen. With the advent of GVHD, a severe rash engulfed me from head to foot, my fingernails and toenails turned brown and died, and the skin on my palms and feet started to peel. My liver and kidney functions were also affected. I was jaundiced, as indicated by the yellowish tint of my eyes, and my feet swelled to twice their normal size.

During late November and early December, my only visitors outside of the family were Dr. Z., April, two residents who knew me from my previous hospitalizations, and members of my church pastoral staff. The nurses feared that I was sinking into depression and closing myself off from the world. Nothing could be further from the truth.

I was in no shape to entertain visitors. The steroids, which I took to control my GVHD, kept me up every night. During the day, I was taking so many antinausea meds and pain killers that I went about in a daze. April later told me that when she visited me in late November, I was devoid of personality. "It wasn't you, Rob," she said. "There was nothing there . . . almost as if you were in a trance. I've never seen anything like it."

She was right. I wasn't myself. Thirty-five pounds underweight, I was so frail that I had to strain just to get up from the toilet. My left side was so sore from the open lung biopsy that I couldn't raise my arm over my head or take a deep breath without pain. On the average, it took me 45 minutes to undress and shower. When I was done, the nurses wrapped me in a pre-heated blanket to keep me from catching a chill. I often wondered if bathing were worth the effort. Entertaining visitors and talking on the phone become less of a priority when it takes all you have to maintain your personal hygiene. I was so physically and mentally shell-shocked from my BMT experience that even praying took effort. For the next month, I relied on the prayers of others and my mom's reading the Bible to me because I was in too much of a narcotic fog to pray for myself. In those days, an encouraging letter or greeting card sometimes made a more lasting impression on me than a phone call or visit because I could re-read it later and the memory wouldn't fade once the drugs wore off.

As bad as I felt, I still expected to be home by Christmas. In fact, my mom and I talked about having one of my friends come over to celebrate the holiday festivities with us because he had no family of his own. Unfortunately, my ordeal was far from over.

I've battled travelers diarrhea in both Thailand and Ghana, but nothing could have prepared me for December '93. When Acute GVHD set its claim on my GI system the week after Thanksgiving, the three-fold defense of the corticosteroid *Solu-Medrol,* the immunosuppressant *Cyclosporine,* and the antidiarrheal medication *Sandistatin* seemed powerless in its wake. At one point, the diarrhea became so unrelenting that I averaged 3-5 liters a day.

In my condition, the slightest ingestion of food or water caused gastrointestinal distress. Dr. R. took me off all solid food, including my beloved popsicles, and she insisted that I only drink water when I took my oral medications. To keep my throat from becoming so parched by the dry air on the unit, she wrote me a prescription for artificial saliva (yes, such a thing does exist).

"Robert, this may seem like a setback, but this is exactly what I want to see," Dr. R. assured me. "You need some GVHD to insure that we cure you of your disease. After all you've been through, it would be a shame for you to have another relapse."

"I know," I answered, but my heart wasn't in it. Just four days earlier, I'd graduated from cream of wheat to turkey and mashed potatoes. My esophagus was still sensitive, but I was starting to tolerate real food. Dr. F., the BMT physician on-call that Thanksgiving was so pleased that she raised the possibility of taking me off TPN for good. Now it looked as if I might be on it indefinitely.

I wanted to get out of that hospital and move on with the rest of my life. Dr. R.'s contention that I needed the GVHD to provide a defense against a leukemic relapse did little to lift my spirits. Depressed and angry, I just sat in my room and sulked.

Two days later, my mom told me a story which turned my attitude around 180 degrees. "Rob, I just finished talking with the father of a BMT patient who was admitted today," she said. "I think you may want to hear about this."

"Okay," I said.

"Well, she's a young woman from Russia who received a BMT for acute leukemia three years ago," she explained. "From what he told me, she breezed through her transplant, had no problems with GVHD whatsoever, and now she's relapsed. What do you think about that?"

"She relapsed after three years?" I asked. "How's she doing right now?"

"Oh, she's upset," she replied. "Wouldn't you be upset if you were in her shoes?"

"Of course," I said.

"Rob, do you realize how fortunate you are?" she asked. "Who's to say you don't need this GVHD to defend against a second relapse? Only God knows what it takes to cure you. Dr. R. and the rest of them can only go by statistics. Frankly, I'm glad that you're having so much GVHD because it serves as a confirmation that

God is going to heal you.

"Now be honest," she continued. "Wouldn't you always question whether you're really healed if you just breezed through everything with little or no GVHD?"

"Probably," I admitted.

"Well, her story ought to put your whole experience here in perspective," she said. "God's not letting anything escape his notice."

"Yeah, I know," I agreed. "Are they going to give her another transplant?"

"Her father didn't say," she said. "Oh, I almost forgot. Guess who her hematologist is."

"Dr. Z.?" I asked.

"Yes, and she thinks he's wonderful, just like us," she said with a smile.

I never met this particular patient, and I often wonder what happened to her. Hearing her story gave me the resolve to endure the present discomfort of my GVHD and admit for the umpteenth time that God's timing was superior to mine.

CHAPTER XXI

One Step Forward,
Two Steps Back

As November blended into December, I fought day-in and day-out to keep myself from going "stir crazy." Thankfully, I didn't have to fight that battle on my own. Every day my mom came and stayed with me until dinner time, and my dad never failed to come by the hospital after work. On weekends, David, Brenda, or Maj often came by as well.

During the first week of December, the BMT staff discovered the incisions on my back were not healing, a side-effect caused by the steroid Solu-Medrol. Three weeks had passed since my open lung biopsy, and they should have healed by then. By mid-December, they started bleeding, and I began feeling outside air seep in and out of the largest wound whenever I coughed or sneezed.

In an attempt to reverse this problem, the nurses began packing my wounds twice a day with thin, sterile strips of dressing that were soaked in a saline solution. Knowing this problem wasn't going to go away any time soon, the bone marrow doctors tried to reduce my steroid dosage and control my diarrhea with the IV drug *Antithymocyte Globulin (ATG)*. Because ATG is notorious for causing deep bone pain, Dr. J., who had taken over for Dr. R. on the first of December, assured me that it would be discontinued if I had difficulty tolerating it.

At first glance, the new drug appeared to be very effective in controlling my diarrhea. Two days after the first infusion, my diarrhea tapered enough for me resume eating and drinking.

"We'll start you off on liquids, such as beef or chicken broth to make sure your GI system is capable of absorbing nutrients," Dr. J. said.

"Do you think my GVHD is improving?" I asked.

"Well, that remains to be seen. You need to abstain from all dairy products and eat only bland, low-fiber foods such as rice, cream of wheat, or noodles until we're sure your gut can tolerate them," he answered.

"No problem," I said.

I longed for the time I could eat pizza, tacos, and Chinese food again, but my GI system had been through the wringer. I didn't need any more setbacks.

"Hopefully, we'll be able to give you an early Christmas present by discharging you in a couple of weeks," Dr. J. added.

"That would be great!" I said.

A few days later, a water pipe burst at the end of the hallway, contaminating several rooms on the unit. To insure the safety of the patients in those rooms, they were moved down to my end of the hall. Although my parents had just finished decorating my room for Christmas, Dr. J. decided to transfer me to the oncology floor to make my room available for someone else. Although it may be hard to believe, I was considered one of the healthier patients on the unit.

When my dad heard I would be moved to the oncology floor, he opposed the idea. "I don't think leaving the bone marrow unit is in your best interest at all," he said.

"Dad, we have no choice," I countered. "They need my room for some guy who hasn't even had his transplant yet. Besides, the doctors think I'm doing real well. Dr. J. said I might be home by Christmas."

"Rob, I saw what you went through last month," he stated. "I just can't sit back and let my son be exposed to untold dangers that might occur because you're not being monitored by the nurses on this floor. As for being discharged before Christmas, I wouldn't hold out much hope."

"Now Dave, wait a minute," my mom said. "We have to believe God is in control here. Look, Dr. J. knows what he's doing. He's known Rob since he was first diagnosed with leukemia. If you recall, he's a regular member of the hematology team, and his wife is the chief nurse of oncology with the Lombardi Cancer Research Center."

"Yeah, and Dr. J. has been the inpatient doctor in charge of my case in the past," I added. "He was the attending physician on-call during my third round of chemotherapy a year ago, and Dr. Z. trusts him."

"Well, it's not Dr. J. that I'm so concerned about," he said. "Rob, you may be feeling better, but in my opinion, moving you to the oncology floor is a big mistake. The wounds on your back haven't healed, and you still need nurses to pack the largest one morning and night.

"All this talk about discharging you before Christmas is premature," he continued. "I don't think they should let you out of this hospital until that back is healed. Even if home IV care is available, it's not worth the risk. You're still dependent on platelet and blood transfusions, TPN, and umpteen other IV medications, several of which are unfamiliar to most nurses."

"Well, we just have to trust God and believe that he won't let me be discharged before I'm ready. As for my being moved to the oncology floor, I know those nurses and have the utmost confidence in them," I said.

"We've got to have faith that God isn't going to let something happen to Rob," my mom said. "I'm not wild about him leaving the BMT unit either, but I know God will look out for him. He always has in the past."

My dad was right to a large degree. The wounds on my back were not healed, and there were no guarantees that my diarrhea wouldn't return for an encore. That said, I resented his "gloom and doom" mentality.

During my first three days on the oncology unit, I experienced little diarrhea and felt enough energy to walk the hallways several times a day. For the first time in eight weeks, I resumed talking on the phone. The festive Christmas decorations in my room gave me even more of a lift. My front wall was tapered with garland and Christmas cards, and I even had a ceramic Christmas tree by my bedside. As far as my eating was concerned, Dr. J. limited me to bland, starchy foods, but I was taking it one day at a time. I was convinced that in no time at all, I would be sitting at our dining table and feasting on a Christmas dinner of turkey, ham, green beans, and mashed potatoes with gravy.

I knew Dad was wrong. I haven't felt this well since I began TBI.

I couldn't wait to get home. I missed seeing my friends and playing with Graycee, whose picture was back on the front wall of my hospital room as it had been in July '92. My optimism had to be tempered, however, with concern over my incisions. My doctors consulted the Departments of Thoracic Surgery and Plastic Surgery in the hopes of finding a solution to what had become a major health risk. My dad told me months later that when the surgeons shone their lights into my largest wound that evening, the outside of my left lung could be seen.

During my fourth night on the oncology floor, I started to experience nausea, abdominal cramping, and bloody diarrhea. The next morning, my entire digestive system "shut down." My abdomen became so distended that I looked pregnant. When my mom saw me that morning, she said, "I don't think you should eat your breakfast until a doctor checks this out. I'll bet you haven't digested a thing in the past 24 hours."

Over the next two hours, several residents came in to examine me, and they were dumbfounded. They tried to listen to my stomach for bowel sounds and heard nothing. Suspecting the onset of a serious GI problem, they transferred me back to the BMT unit and consulted a gastroenterologist.

Still haunted by the memories of my open lung biopsy and five weeks of isolation, I didn't want to go anywhere near the BMT unit until I knew for certain I'd walk out those double doors the same day. I imagined myself returning months later with no mask over my face and no unsteadiness in my gait. I was going to be the conquering hero the next time the nurses saw me; the poster boy for the whole BMT program. A return to the scene of the crime just four days after I left hit me where it hurts: my pride.

Dad was right. I'm in no shape to go home any time soon. Every time I take a step forward in my recovery, something happens to set me behind for weeks. God, this is getting old! I don't know what you're up to here, but I'll be lucky to make it out of here by the end of January.

Stress and the fear of the unknown defined the next 72 hours. In addition to my latest GI problems, my breathing became so labored that I felt as if a huge weight had just been placed on my chest. Although they didn't know for certain, the BMT staff suspected that either GVHD had invaded my lungs, or I'd contracted an infection. Although they couldn't make a diagnosis based on my symptoms alone, they believed the culprit might be the dreaded *Cytomegalovirus (CMV)*, a potentially fatal disease caused by a variant of the herpes virus.[1]

When Dr. J. apprised me of my medical status that Sunday afternoon, I'd never seen a doctor look so sullen. At this point, neither GVHD or CMV had a favorable prognosis. The stratospheric levels of steroids I'd been taking the past month had already caused major complications with my surgical wounds. A spread of GVHD to the lungs meant an even higher dosage of steroids, thus exacerbating the problem with my wounds and increasing the likelihood of infection.

As for CMV, the most effective treatment is the combination of *CMV-Immune Gamma Globulin* and *Gancyclovir*, a powerful antiviral agent. Unfortunately, a common side-effect of this treatment is the reduction of white cells in the blood and marrow.[2] My donor and I both tested negative for CMV prior to my transplant, but there was no guarantee that I hadn't been exposed to it since then, despite precautions taken by the nurses.[3]

Post-transplant infections must be treated immediately if the patient has any hope of surviving. Since it takes several days to confirm the presence of CMV, the BMT staff scheduled me for a colonoscopy that afternoon and a CAT scan of my lungs and

---

[1] National Cancer Institute, *Research Report: Bone Marrow Transplant, 1991 Edition*, 24.

[2] Leukemia Society of America, *Bone Marrow Transplantation (BMT)* (New York: Leukemia Society of America, 1992) 27.

[3] Fifty percent of the public have been exposed to CMV, but it usually remains dormant and is only activated during periods of extreme immunosuppression. To reduce my risk for contracting CMV, the BMT nurses always provided me with CMV negative blood products. National Cancer institute, *Research Report: Bone Marrow Transplant, 1991 Edition*, 24.

abdomen the next evening to rule out GVHD first.[4] They reasoned that if my tests came back negative for GVHD, they could blast me with a broad array of IV medications, including those used to treat CMV.

Following my meeting with Dr. J., David came by for a visit. Because he and Brenda were going to spend Christmas with her parents in Idaho, he gave me my present a week early. Seeing how poorly I felt, he didn't stay long. After I thanked him for the gift, he went to the BMT waiting room where my mom was talking with Dr. J.

"Mom, I'm scared," he said. "Should Brenda and I cancel our trip?"

"No," she replied. "You and Brenda need to continue on with your plans to visit her family. There's nothing you can do here anyhow. We'll call you if anything develops."

At a loss over what to do next, Dr. J. slumped down into a chair next to her and sighed, "I don't know what else I can do."

In a response of faith, my mom said, "Doctors can treat illness, but only God can heal. We just have to put Rob in God's hands and trust him to complete the work."

He agreed.

---

[4] A colonoscopy is a procedure in which the inner lining of the colon and the large intestine can be observed via a long, lighted tube (known as a colonoscope) and biopsied using a pair of long forceps. *The Signet Mosby Medical Encyclopedia*, Rev. ed. (New York: Penguin Books USA Inc., 1996), 190.

CHAPTER XXII

Joy Comes in the Morning

No one verbalized their fears in my presence, but everyone, including my parents, feared I might not recover from this latest setback. When my dad came home that Sunday night after visiting me, he told my mom, "You know, he might not make it."

As for myself, I was so determined to live that I refused to consider the worst possible scenario. I'm not an objective judge on how often I've crossed the line between faith and presumption. However, when Dr. J. first told me the bleak news about my health status, I just "knew" this wouldn't be the end. Sure, I was frustrated, weary of fighting, and anxious over what I might face over the next several days. Nevertheless, I wasn't about to concede defeat, and I became annoyed at some of the residents under Dr. J.'s care because I could tell they didn't share my confidence.

When the orderly came to take me down for my CAT scan the following evening, I was so weak I needed help climbing onto the gurney. My spirits received a huge lift, however, when I was greeted by a familiar figure in the Department of Radiology waiting room. It was Pastor Ahlemann, Senior Pastor of CFC. I didn't expect to see him there, but apparently, he'd stopped by the hospital after going to see the National Christmas Tree with his son. I can't remember what he said to me, but it wouldn't have mattered anyway. Just seeing him there gave me a boost of calm assurance that I would be alright. I knew, without a doubt, God wasn't finished with me yet because he was still putting me on the hearts and minds of others.

The way I felt when I saw my pastor that evening is a microcosm of the impact loved ones, friends, and even total strangers had on my emotional well-being as a patient. My most precious memories from my BMT experience were the times people did the unexpected on my behalf. Our church was one of the largest churches in northern Virginia, and yet Pastor Ahlemann visited me at least once a week. Before my diagnosis, I was just a graduate student who popped in and out every Christmas and Summer break. Outside of an occasional handshake in the Sunday morning greeting line, he didn't know me.

My pastor is one among many who were used by God to bring encouragement into my life. The pastors of several other churches in the area, many of whom didn't know me personally, prayed for me during their church services on a regular basis. If that were not enough prayer support, my grandmother's pastor in Greensboro, NC prayed for me every morning during his radio broadcast!

This outpouring of compassion wasn't limited to church leaders. Knowing my parents were so preoccupied with looking after me, several of my friends from church brought food to our home. The day after Pastor Ahlemann's visit, two of my mom's sisters, Juanita and Betty, came up from North Carolina to clean our house, cook several meals, and pay me a visit. Throughout my ordeal at Georgetown, my Aunt Sandy (the youngest of my mom's three sisters) sent me encouraging get-well cards on a weekly basis. True to her nature, she never missed a holiday or special occasion, whether it was my birthday, Thanksgiving, or Christmas.

As for medical personnel, Dr. Z. checked up on me several times, despite the fact I was no longer under his care. Others who touched my life in a similar way include, but are not limited to, several young residents whom I had come to know during the course of my treatments, two Christian radiologists who lifted my spirits every morning as they took my chest X-rays, and Sister Jeanne, the floor chaplain, who was a source of support throughout my stay in the hospital.

Tuesday morning, my prospects took a sudden turn for the better. Dr. J. couldn't hide his elation when he reported the results of my colonoscopy and CAT scan. "The results of your colonoscopy were negative for GVHD, and the CAT scan of your lungs shows no signs of infection or damage," he said.

"Really?" I asked.

"Well, that's certainly good news," my mom said.

"Yes," he replied. "Your recent lung problems are being caused by the pressure of your distended gut on your rib cage, and a partially collapsed left lung," he added. "Outside air is seeping through your large surgical wound and putting pressure on your lung."

"I've suspected outside air might be seeping through there for quite some time," I said.

"We're going to address that problem," Dr. J. assured me, nodding. "The nurses are going to pack your chest wounds three times a day. Hopefully, that will accelerate your healing."

Several days later, my blood cultures confirmed Dr. J.'s conclusions. Dr. N, the gastroenterologist monitoring my case, stated that my severe abdominal cramping and bloody diarrhea were largely caused by the IV medication ATG. Although it may have reduced my output of diarrhea, long-term use of the drug caused constriction and bleeding in my large intestines. The BMT staff discontinued the ATG and hooked me up to a rectal pump for two days to clear out my intestines, but despite my improved prognosis, no one detected bowel sounds with a stethoscope for another two weeks.

The medical staff breathed easier as I approached Christmas Eve, but I was still in poor health. When Betty and Juanita visited me Wednesday morning, I was 55 pounds underweight and the incisions on my back bled so often that platelet and blood transfusions had become a daily ritual. Nevertheless, as my aunts were leaving the hospital, Betty turned to my mom and said, "During our drive up here, we were apprehensive about Robby. We didn't know what to expect. Now that we've seen him, I just know God is going to heal him."

CHAPTER XXIII

A Christmas Blessing

The morning after my aunts' visit, Roxanne, the nurse who had been in charge of my care the previous evening, poked her head into my room and said, "Merry Christmas, Rob! I'll see you in the New Year!"

Merry Christmas.

Since my childhood, I've heard and said those words every year, often forgetting that Christmas isn't merry for everyone. Several years ago, one friend told me he hated the holidays because they reminded him that he didn't have a close-knit family with whom he could share intimate moments over roasted turkey and hot cider. I couldn't relate because I'd never been there. My main worries during the Holiday Season were making sure my airline luggage arrived at National Airport instead of Dulles International and fretting over how well I performed on my semester finals. When my family traveled on Christmas Day, finding an open gas station and a place for lunch topped our concerns. I never gave thought to the fact that the hospitals remain open and crowded 365 days a year.

When Roxanne said, "Merry Christmas, Rob," it was the first time in my life that those words sounded out of place.

Merry for you, perhaps. Not me.

As I lay there in my bed waiting for the day nurse to disconnect my rectal pump, I found little reason to be merry. Spending

Christmas in the hospital was anathema to me. For weeks, "I just want to get out of here by Christmas" had been my creed.

"Rob, Christmas is the same whether you're in the hospital or at home," my dad said. "You can celebrate the birth of Christ anywhere. Even in the hospital."

"Yeah, I know," I said, but my expectations were low.

As it turns out, Christmas '93 was my most blessed in memory. The holidays have always been an occasion for me to strengthen family ties and renew old friendships, but in the past, I took those moments for granted. Christmas '93 showed me that Roxanne and my Dad were right. Although I was unable to go shopping for gifts or send out greeting cards, the people who meant the most in my life brought Christmas to me. I received so many cards and letters, some from as far away as California, that my front wall was plastered with a rich array of green, gold, and red. Several visitors besides my parents came by the hospital to spread their good will, even on Christmas Day. To top it all off, I liked every article of clothing I received.

The most meaningful event of that Holiday Season occurred on the evening of Christmas Day. After talking to David long-distance in Idaho, I tried in vain to reach my grandmother in North Carolina. Just after I hung up the phone, however, I received a long-distance call from Tommy, the cousin who visited me in November. Expecting to have the coherent conversation we both missed when I was in a narcotic fog six weeks earlier, I was surprised by singing. Many of my relatives from my mom's side of the family had gathered at Betty's home, and at Tommy's cue, they broke into a chorus of "We wish you a merry Christmas and a happy New Year."

Some of the fondest memories from my childhood — joint vacations to the beach, Christmas Eve at Grandma's, excursions to the mountains of West Virginia — were spent in the company of my extended family. As my cousins and I grew older, our priorities changed, our lives became complicated, and the times we saw one another became few and far between. Many of us went off to college. The rest of us found full-time jobs or got married. By the time I left for graduate school, I felt a real void in my life because my relationship with them was based more on memories than anything else.

My diagnosis with leukemia brought us closer than we'd been in years. During my time in the hospital, not a week went by when I didn't receive a card, letter, or phone call from one of them. In that past year, I saw some of them more often than I did during the previous six years combined. Not being able to celebrate the holiday festivities with them this year saddened me more than the prospect of spending Christmas Day in the hospital.

When they finished serenading me, they got on the phone to talk with me. Three aunts, two uncles, five cousins, four second cousins and one grandmother later, tears were streaming down my face. I wasn't there in person, but I've never felt as close to them as I did at that moment.

I believe this event changed me as a person. Somewhere between late childhood and young adulthood, I bought into the idea that a reserved, controlled demeanor was a sign of strength and emotional outbursts were a sign of instability. I'm optimistic by nature, but there have been many times in my life when I've adopted a calm exterior to mask feelings of anxiety or insecurity. During the darkest days of my BMT experience, I put a positive spin on my condition whenever I spoke with doctors and visitors. When my friend John called me from Saudi Arabia in early November to ask me if the reports of my pneumonia were true, I blew my lung problems off as a minor glitch that was improving day by day. I didn't lie to him intentionally, but I felt like I had to hold onto whatever silver lining I found, even if it didn't exist.

My graduate school experience helped me get more in touch with feelings like anger and resentment, but to be honest, I never came close to resolving those emotions until after my leukemia diagnosis. Even after I learned to own up to feelings such as anger or jealousy, crying in front of others or admitting my fears still embarrassed me. I've never found it difficult to hug people and say the words "I love you," but Christmas Day '93 was the first time in my life that I cried openly because I had been so touched by the love I received from others.

When I finished talking on the phone with my relatives, my dad said, "Rob, I don't think I've seen you cry like that since your childhood."

"Really?" I said.

"I think that your doing so shows significant growth and maturity," he said. "Since I've known you, you've never responded like that."

A life-threatening illness can spawn personal maturity in many ways, including the maturity that says, "I'm not embarrassed to show others I'm human, loving, and vulnerable."

CHAPTER XXIV

Touched by the Death
of a Stranger

===

As I approached New Year's Day '94, I wondered if my stay in the hospital would last the entire winter. I stopped projecting when I would finally be released because to date, nothing had gone as I'd expected. My October prediction that I would be discharged by Thanksgiving was laughable in retrospect. Except for the plain pasta and cream of wheat I'd eaten two weeks earlier, I hadn't tasted a bite of real food since Thanksgiving weekend.

In spite of everything that had gone wrong, I still had reason to be thankful. The love and support of friends and family engulfed me, and as far as my health was concerned, things could have been worse. I know for a fact they were for some of the other patients on my floor.

One such patient, Carol, stayed right across the hall. A few days after Christmas, I noticed a frantic buzz of activity as doctors and nurses poured in and out of her room. "What's going on?" I asked Jean, the nurse in charge of my care.

"We're trying to stabilize the woman across the hall," she replied.

"Are they having any success?" I asked.

"No." she sighed.

I didn't press for details because it wasn't any of my business.

Jean's pressured speech told me the entire story anyway.

She's dying.

I waited until the evening to go for my walk on the BMT corridor because I didn't want to get in the way of the medical personnel gathered around her door. When I finally ventured out of my room, the hallway was empty except for a priest who was consoling some of her family members. I knew then that she didn't make it.

For the next few days, a thick cloud covered an already gloomy place. The doctors and nurses who fought to prolong Carol's life were silent and crestfallen. As their profession dictated, however, they put her death behind them and tended to the needs of the living.

They cleaned her room. They took the sign bearing her name off the door. By the time another patient had moved into her room, it was as if she'd never existed.

Life went on like nothing had happened. The weather didn't change, people still went to work, and Tom Brokaw never mentioned her during his evening broadcast. Carol's death served as a startling reminder of how the death of one person is a trivial matter to the rest of the world.

Thank God no one is a trivial statistic in his eyes.

I couldn't help asking the question, *Could I be next?* I'd trusted God for my healing from the day I began treatment, but now I wondered if my faith had been wishful thinking.

The day after Carol died, I asked my parents, "Do you still believe I'll be healed? I mean, I know we've all claimed that I'll be healed 'totally and completely,' but how can we be sure we're not just fooling ourselves?"

"Rob," my mom said, "I know as surely as I know my name that it's God's will to heal you. When you were real sick a week ago, I asked God, 'Did we hear you correctly?'"

My dad chimed in, "When I arrived home from the hospital the night Dr. J. said you may have GVHD in your lungs, I said to your mother, 'He might not make it.'"

"But, Rob," my mom added, "When he said that, I felt something rising within me that said, *'No! God will heal him!'*

"It's different with you, and I knew it before we landed in L.A. last year," she stated. "Don't you remember what Catherine Marshall's book said about relinquishing our needs to God?"[1]

"I remember you telling me about it," I said.

"Well, while I was reading it, God showed me something I'll never forget: the difference between striving and trusting," she continued. "When God told me I was striving when I asked him to heal my brother Bill, I released you to his care. At that moment, I came to terms with Bill's death, and I concluded that his illness and yours didn't parallel.

"Remember the scripture God gave me the night before we flew out to California: 'And we know that in all things God works for the good of those who love him, who have been called according to his purpose?'" she asked.[2]

"Yes," I said.

"Rob, we don't need to strive to get God to answer us," she explained. "He knows our needs before we ask, and if it's his will to do something, he gives us the faith to believe it will come to pass. After God revealed that to me, I turned to your father and told him, 'He's going to beat it.'"

My dad added, "Everything that has happened since you were diagnosed, including the way we found a teaching hospital like Georgetown without health insurance, the message Melanie left on your phone machine, and the numerous words of encouragement regarding your healing, has confirmed it's God's will to heal you."

"Rob," my mom said, "even when things have looked bad, like the open lung biopsy or the recent problems with your intestines, the best of all scenarios has been the result."

She was right. The patient across the hall was **not** me.

---

[1] See Chapter 5
[2] Romans 8:28

CHAPTER XXV

New Year's Day '94

Saturday, January 1, was a real turning point in my walk of faith. That afternoon, I received the most visitors to date. Phil and Carolyn, my parents' Sunday school teachers at CFC, came shortly after breakfast, followed by Maj and several close friends of the family. Accompanying Maj was Bob, an elder at Burke Community Church, where our family came to faith in Christ two decades earlier. As Bob and the others laid their hands on me, he received the following "word from the Lord" concerning me:

> *"Walk in my peace and my joy; not the world's, but mine. You are my child and you have a calling on your life. You shall know my healing power."*

Those words have been imprinted on my mind forever. When they were spoken, I needed to be reassured that it was God's will to heal me. It wasn't as if my parents' encouraging words a few days earlier didn't bolster my faith, but in the same way a child needs his parents to remind him of their love after he's had a rough day, I needed God to reassure me that I wasn't going to expire any time soon.

"Walk in my peace and my joy; not the world's, but mine." The world's idea of peace is the absence of conflict; the calm after the storm. In times of such peace, joy abounds. When our soldiers

returned home after World War II, the people danced in Times Square. They didn't dance after the *Challenger* disaster. The world's peace and joy are fleeting. The peace of God is the calm in the midst of the storm. To have his peace is to rest in the knowledge that even when life seems out of control, God hasn't fallen from his throne and can still be trusted to carry you through the darkest moments of life. I'm not talking about a flight into fantasy or a denial of pain. The peace and joy I'm describing is a calm delight in the goodness of God despite the circumstances.

With each setback, I was accumulating a first-class education in what it means to experience God's peace and joy in the face of suffering. That previous October, I entered the LAF room expecting no complications, mild GVHD, and a discharge five weeks later. I never joyfully anticipated adversity as an opportunity to develop character. I wanted to be healed on the spot.

If I'd breezed through my BMT and been discharged before Christmas, I would have given myself most of the credit. Others would have as well. My Aunt Betty told my mom one day that if I hadn't gone through all the struggles of the past two months, she would have said, "Well, Robby's a fighter. You can't keep that Brown constitution down for long, now can you?" Bob's word of knowledge set the record straight.

Bob and Maj's visit was just the beginning of the watershed experience I had that day. Later on, several other close friends of the family came by and prayed for my protection from infection. As they were praying, I envisioned a protective canopy coming down and covering me from head to foot. I don't know whether this classifies as a "vision," but I knew from then on that God had just answered their prayers in the affirmative.

Toward the end of their visit, our friend Elaine gave me the same encouragement that Jeremiah had for the Israelites when they were in captivity:

> "For I know the plans I have for you," declares the LORD, "plans to prosper you and not to harm you, plans to give you hope and a future. Then you will call upon me and come and pray to me, and I will listen to you. You will seek me and find me when you seek me with all your heart."[1]

My brother David had given me that same scripture passage weeks earlier, so I knew it was meant for me.

My condition didn't dramatically improve that afternoon. I still couldn't eat solid food, and the nurses continued packing the wound on my back. However, as New Year's Day '94 drew to a close, I knew I just took a major step in my return to complete health. My heart and spirit were so renewed that my perspective couldn't have been anything but positive.

---

[1] Jeremiah 29:11-13

CHAPTER XXVI

Ken

========================

During the first week of January, I received an unexpected guest.

"Rob, are you up for visitors?" a familiar voice asked.

"Sure," I answered. "Who is it?"

"It's me, Joyce," she replied as she poked her head into the doorway.

Joyce was the Oncology/BMT Social Worker. I first met her in June '92, and she had a smile on her face every time I saw her. She's the kind of person you want to have as a hospital social worker because she lifts the spirits of everyone around her.

"Come on in," I said.

"I have someone here who would like to meet you," she said. "This is Ken, a former patient here. When I told him about you, he asked if he could talk with you."

After introducing himself, he told me that he had a BMT for acute leukemia in 1991.

"How long were you in the hospital?" I asked.

"I was here for a total of six months," he replied. "It wasn't all at once though. I was discharged after my marrow engrafted, but I later returned because of problems with GVHD."

"How bad was it?" I asked.

"It got so bad I had to have part of my large intestine removed and a colostomy done so I could pass my waste products," he said.

"At one point, the doctor told me he couldn't do anything more for me."

"Boy, what I'm going through is mild in comparison to what you experienced." I said. "Did you receive your transplant from a family member or was it unrelated?"

"My brother was my donor," he replied.

"I wouldn't expect the GVHD to be that bad with a sibling's marrow," I remarked. "Was it a perfect match?"

"Yeah, it was a good match, but he certainly had some strong marrow," he laughed.

Ken's hair had grown back and he no longer wore a face mask, but the effects of his BMT remained. His GI system never returned to normal, even after his intestines were repaired. His liver continued to cause him problems, and he took medications every day to counteract Chronic GVHD. When I met him, he was still on disability and was just beginning to consider returning to work. In spite of his limitations, he expressed a joy for life and an abiding faith in God. Emblazoned in a "Jesus" T-shirt, Ken was a Christian. Before he left, we prayed together.

I saw Ken a year later at a BMT reunion banquet, but that was the last time I ever heard from him. Four years later, a nurse told me he eventually succumbed to the health problems caused by his BMT. Although he's gone home to his reward, his grace in the midst of suffering continues to challenge me to this day.

CHAPTER XXVII

Two Steps Forward, One Step Back

Several days after Ken's visit, additional tests revealed that despite some mild bleeding in my large intestines, my GI system had remarkably improved.

"Rob," my mom said, "I was just talking with Dr. M. He said that if your gut continues to heal, you can resume eating in a few days. He also said, 'We'll discharge him as soon as his back wound closes and he can eat food without a significant increase in diarrhea.' Isn't that great?"

"Yeah. I'm just trusting that God will give him the wisdom to know when it's time to discharge me," I replied.

Toward the end of the second week of January, my daily output of diarrhea tapered off to a half-liter per day. Delighted with my progress, Dr. M. said, "I think we can start you on solid food again. Because your intestines are sensitive, we'll take it slow." Then he asked, "What do you think about us starting you off on Pedialyte tomorrow?" he asked.

"That would be great!" I replied.

For the next two weeks, I resumed the same bland diet of liquids and soft foods I followed in mid-December, adding one item to the menu each day. I made considerable progress, but reintroducing

141

myself to food wasn't easy. My GI system had become so used to going without food that eating no longer seemed like second nature. My main staples of starchy, low fiber foods such as plain pasta, cream of wheat (with 100% Lactaid milk), and rice were so tasteless I often became nauseated at their sight.

I still looked pregnant. Sometimes, I wondered if I'd ever return to normal. I knew I couldn't remain on TPN forever because it was taking a toll on my liver. Worse yet, it didn't put meat back on my bones. Several nights I dreamed about food.

Each time I ate, I followed my parents' advice and viewed the food as medicine. In light of the food I was allowed to eat, their advice made sense. The hospital is the only place where cream of wheat is more conducive to brick laying than eating, noodles taste like styrofoam, and hard boiled egg whites have the consistency of "silly putty." It might just as well have been medicine.

As I approached the end of my third month in the hospital, a great chasm still needed to be crossed before I could go home. I now entertained visitors several times a week and felt strong enough to walk the halls four times a day at 20 minute intervals. However, I still depended on daily infusions of TPN, medications, and blood products. Worse yet, the largest wound on my back hadn't healed, and the surgeons who monitored my progress warned me that additional surgery might be imminent.

During the month of January, I plowed through three novels and saw enough reruns of *Star Trek: The Next Generation* to last a lifetime. No matter how hard I tried to avoid cabin fever, the gap of time between seeing and reaching the light at the end of the tunnel tested my patience. Numerous patients admitted after Thanksgiving had long since completed their treatments and gone home. It seemed as if everyone was leaving the hospital and getting on with life except me. I wanted to go home so bad I could taste it.

Whenever outsiders asked my dad about my progress, he compared it to the stock market. "The general trend is upward, but there's so many fluctuations within a given week that we never know what to expect the next time we see him," he said.

Spending time in prayer and the Word strengthened me more than anything else. Now I had the physical and mental stamina to pray for myself and others. I kept a stack of 3x5 index cards by my bedside, each of which contained a scriptural promise of divine healing or the peace of God.[1] Reading those verses out-loud to myself every night and day strengthened my faith whenever the chasm from here to there seemed insurmountable.

I went through one of those "low periods" the last weekend of January. After two weeks of relative calm, the diarrhea returned. And it was as bloody as ever.

Suspecting either a flare-up of GVHD or bowel irritation, Dr. R. took me off solid food for the rest of the weekend to give my digestive system a rest. Because my upper GI tract was growing accustomed to solid food, going off it "cold turkey" triggered nausea and vomiting.

Disappointed and frustrated, I poured my heart out to God.

God, I don't understand this . . . I asked you to give the doctors wisdom in deciding when to reintroduce me to solid food. I assumed that when I started eating again, it would be uphill from there. Now, it seems as if the progress I've made has been a mirage. I don't see any reason for this at all, and I feel like you're just jerking me around!

As he'd done in the past, God used another human being to cheer me up and help me regain perspective. Allison, a part-time weekend nurse, hadn't seen me since early December. From my standpoint, my improvement went at a snail's pace. In the eyes of one who had last seen me at my worst, it was a different story. My recent problems aside, I was still alive and gaining strength. For instance, although my largest wound still caused me problems, the smaller wound had completely healed. While changing my dressings that Saturday morning, Allison remarked, "Rob, I can see the 'light at the end of the tunnel' you've been refering to."

"Really? How do they look?" I asked.

"The smaller one at the bottom has closed. The large one at the top is still open, but it's coming along," she said.

Being around someone with a positive attitude is contagious. When Allison said she could see the light at the end of the tunnel, my own optimism was rejuvenated.

---

[1] Many of these verses can be found in the Appendix section of this book.

"Yeah," I agreed. "I guess I am doing much better. I think the problems with my gut that I started having yesterday are a minor glitch."

"You're much better than you were in December. I was worried there for awhile," she stated.

"Well," I replied, "I've got to credit God and my faith in him because that's what has pulled me through."

"Rob, I admire you and your faith," she said. "You know . . . the way you've handled this."

The only thing that I could say in return was, "Thanks."

I was encouraged that Allison saw that my faith in God had made a difference in my life. For the first time, I began to see that my extended stay in the hospital may have been, in part, for the benefit of others. I didn't "preach" to everyone who came through my door, but I made no pretension about the source of my strength. Most of the doctors and nurses who took care of me knew my family and I were Christians. Some said they were praying for me.

As for those who were silent, I don't know if they just thought my faith was quaint or a desperate grasp for straws. It didn't matter. I hoped that when I left the unit, people who have never given a thought to God would remember the work he accomplished in my life.

Don't get me wrong. I was far from the "perfect" Christian witness. I wasn't always warm and friendly toward the medical staff, especially when they woke me in the middle of the night to draw blood or take my vital signs. Several times, my mom scolded me for being curt with the surgical residents for taking off my dressings and checking my wounds after the nurses had just finished dressing them. I'm thankful to God that despite my imperfections, he saw fit to demonstrate his grace to others through my life.

CHAPTER XXVIII

Haven't We Been Here Before?

Sunday, January 30 put my upbeat attitude to the test. My largest wound had been packed with sterile, wet-to-dry dressings three times a day for the past month, but outside air continued to put pressure on my left lung. When my morning X-rays showed that my lung had partially collapsed, a surgical resident informed me that a chest tube would be installed if the lung didn't reinflate on its own.

I'll be honest with you," he added. "It's been my experience that chest wounds like yours take a long time to heal. Even if your lung reinflates on its own or by means of a chest tube, this problem will recur as long as that incision remains an open wound. If things don't improve within the next two weeks, we're going to operate."

I didn't want to go under the knife again. It had been the cause of my misery two months earlier, and now it was being touted as the solution. I knew God could heal me without surgery, but that was his domain. Sick and tired of begging God to see things my way, I just placed the matter in his hands. There was nothing else I could do, and I wasn't about to let this latest crisis spoil a date with my friends John and Linda. A newly-wed couple from my church, both of them came by later that night to watch the Cowboys pummel the Bills in Super bowl XXVIII.

Further tests the next day confirmed a collapsed lung, and a chest tube was installed into my left breast via local anesthesia. I was unhappy about being confined to my room for the next several days, until I received the encouraging news that I could eat again. After going without food for three days, my volume of diarrhea had become so negligible that the BMT doctors concluded that my recent flare-up was bowel irritation, not GVHD.

As January gave way to February, I reached one of the most significant milestones BMT patients pass on their journey toward recovery: Day 100. Over the next two weeks, my doctors put me through my Hundred Day Work-up, which consisted of a series of tests identical to the Preliminary BMT Work-up in September.[1] These tests would assess my vital organs and determine if any negative effects of the BMT were reversible. Given my base-line health five months earlier, no one would have predicted that I would go through these tests as an inpatient.

During this time, the BMT doctors tried to taper me off the IV steroids to accelerate the healing of my wound (which remained a gaping hole in my back) so I could avoid surgery. In order to counteract a recurrence of GVHD, Dr. M. prescribed the oral immunosuppressant *Imuran*. Unlike steroids, Imuran doesn't mask infections, raise blood pressure, or inhibit the healing of wounds.

Toward the end of the first week of February, our plans hit a snag. I broke out in an awful skin rash, my worst since early November, and my daily output of diarrhea doubled. This time, there was no denying it. My stools had the tell-tale "dirty motor oil" look of GVHD. Worse yet, my left lung hadn't improved over the past two weeks, and we were running out of options. Dr. G., the head of Thoracic Surgery, was opposed to performing surgery while I was still on the steroids, but it was obvious to everyone that he might have to operate under less than optimal conditions.

On the night of Feb. 12, Dr. G came by my room to inform me that my latest X-ray indicated that my left lung had now collapsed in two different places.

"What does that mean?" I asked.

"We're going to have to operate," he replied. "We plan to use some of the flesh from the front of your chest cavity to fill in the

---

[1] See Chapter XVI.

open wound in the back. In the meantime, we're going to put a chest tube into your backside to reinflate your lung."

"What about **this** chest tube?" I asked, refering to the chest tube that had been implanted into my left breast two weeks earlier.

"We're going to keep it for now," he said.

After Dr. G. had left, my dad stated, "Rob, I don't think you'll need this surgery. Now, I've been praying about this for quite some time, and I believe God will heal you on his own."

"I know he can do it, Dad, but the question is whether he will or not," I said.

"The open lung biopsy got you into this mess in the first place," my dad countered. "Now they're talking about doing surgery again to correct the problem? I don't think that's God's will," he said.

"I hope you're right," I sighed.

I didn't want to get my hopes up by saying I wouldn't need surgery because I knew I couldn't dictate how God should heal me. Besides, it seemed as if the thoracic surgeons had already made up their minds. I resigned myself to just let things happen and believe that God would have his way regardless of what avenue the doctors chose.

God, you're not making this easy are you?

CHAPTER XXIX

What a Difference a Day Makes!

The next morning, prayer chains across the nation buzzed with the news of my impending surgery. In addition to calling our home church prayer chain, my parents notified Breakthrough Ministries, the 700 Club, and the Abundant Life Prayer Group at ORU of my condition. Their collective prayers were answered in dramatic fashion.

That evening, the surgical resident who was supposed to install my next chest tube came through my door carrying two X-rays.

"Are you going to put the second chest tube in?" I asked.

Breaking into a wide smile, he said, "I don't think that's going to be necessary. Your X-ray from this morning shows that your left lung almost completely reinflated over night. Let me show you the films."

Pulling out the two films he was carrying, he said, "This is your X-ray from yesterday morning." Using his finger to show me the differences, he asked, "You see these two dark areas, one up here in the corner and the other, down here at the bottom? These were the places where your lung was collapsed. Now, here is the X-ray from today. See the difference?"

"Yes. But don't we still need to do the surgery?" I asked.

"I don't think so," he replied. "It looks as if your wound may be closing to the point that there's no more outside air seeping through and putting pressure on your lung."

"Whenever I move around, though, I still feel some vibrating back there," I said.

After examining the site of the wound and asking me to cough, he said, "Well, there's no air going through there now."

Later that evening, his diagnosis was confirmed by Dr. G. himself. The chest tube was removed, surgery was deemed unnecessary, and I was ecstatic. One of the oncology residents, Dr. P., attributed my turn of fortune to "divine intervention." Dr. M. said, "Rob, it looks as if all the praying you've been doing has worked!"

The end of the tunnel came within striking distance in a matter of 24 hours. A day earlier, I was facing invasive surgery. Now my doctors were talking about a discharge before the end of the month. That weekend, Dr. M. doubled my steroid dosage, and within a few days, my rash disappeared and my diarrhea stopped. Dr. M. gave me the green light to resume eating and transferred me to the oncology floor. "Provided that you continue to improve," Dr. M. informed me, "we'll discharge you from the hospital on Thursday or Friday."

As elated as I felt over the possibility of being discharged, my parents were apprehensive about my going home in such a weakened condition. And they had reason. The wound on my back was healing, but it still needed to be redressed once a day. Moreover, I remained dependent on TPN, IV doses of Cyclosporine and steroids, and blood and platelet transfusions, which meant that home infusion and nursing services would remain a necessity for several weeks.

My parents' reservations notwithstanding, I was discharged on February 25, 1994. It had been exactly 131 days since I last walked through the front doors of Georgetown University Medical Center, and the news of my discharge was met with a thunder of applause at a Lombardi Cancer Research Center staff meeting. Despite the beating my body had endured over the past four months, God had been true to his character. The results of my Hundred Day Work-up showed that with the exception of minor scaring on my lungs, my inner organs were normal.

The day I said my goodbyes to everyone, some of the nurses from both the oncology floor and BMT unit threw me a party. Their card said it all: "It's been a long road . . . Good luck."

CHAPTER XXX

Home Sweet Home

═══════════════════════════════════════

When I walked into the foyer of our home for the first time since that previous October, I felt a mixture of elation, relief, and uncertainty. I wanted to savor the moment, but I knew the slightest hint of an infection or outbreak of GVHD would land me back in the hospital. On the heels of my first taste of freedom in four months, that prospect seemed worse than never being discharged in the first place.

My parents were even more pensive. They had gone through the ups and downs of the past four months with me, and their nerves were frazzled. The last thing they needed was another crisis because this time, there were no nurses or physicians at our beckoning call.

I was in far worse shape than when I came home after my first round of chemotherapy in July '92. I weighed 135 pounds, and I'd just started eating solid food. I caught a chill at the slightest variance of temperature and required a portable heater near me at all times. Barely able to climb the stairs without assistance, I lacked the stamina to attend to anything beyond my personal hygiene. I remained dependent on daily infusions of TPN, Cyclosporine, and Solu-Medrol, and I took enough oral medications to fill a pharmaceutical inventory.

My immune system resembled that of an infant. I had little defense against the common cold, and my medical history from birth to age 26 was now irrelevant. I no longer enjoyed protection against Tetanus, Diptheria, Polio, the Mumps, Rubella, the Measles, or Small Pox, and my bout with Chicken Pox at the age of five meant nothing. I was starting from scratch.

The health guidelines I followed as a BMT patient continued to apply at home. Fresh fruit and vegetables would be excluded from my diet until six months post-transplant. Everything I put into my mouth needed to be prepackaged, microwaved, or broiled to a crisp. Whenever I ventured outdoors, I wore a mask.

Of all the infections feared by my doctors, fungal infections topped the list. Since these infections flourish in standing water, animal feces, poor ventilation, and excessive dust, my parents banned all houseplants and took extra care to insure the cleanliness of our home. Although we already had an electrostatic air filter on our furnace and a portable air filter in my bedroom, my dad purchased two hepa filters for the basement and family room. I avoided going into the garage without a mask, and I stayed out of the basement until my parents cleaned, washed, and vacuumed it from top to bottom.

When I first came home, I assumed life would get easier now that I was out of the hospital.

No more X-rays, no more entourages of doctors every afternoon, and no more routines dictated by others. Just me, my parents, the dog, and the TV set.

I couldn't have been more naive. Life became hectic the moment I stepped foot in our house. My parents and I spent our waking hours trying to accommodate and communicate with three distinct entities: INOVA home nursing care, outpatient infusion services, and Georgetown Hospital. My mom reports that my first week home was the most stressful of my entire BMT experience. The influx of nurses and medical personnel into our home every morning and night created so much confusion that even Graycee was affected. Although outgoing and friendly with most people, the sight of so many strangers invading our home so unnerved her that she often hid behind the TV set until they left.

This is no different than being in the hospital. Only the location has changed.

For the next three weeks, I adhered to a routine. I **hate** routines unless they're self-imposed. I resumed caring for my catheter, practiced breathing exercises every 30 minutes, gave blood samples every morning, had my vital signs taken twice a day, and planned my life around the schedule of an outpatient case manager. Since portable IV machines were unavailable, I was confined to the upstairs every night from 6:30 p.m. to bedtime. If my friends wanted to visit, they often did so on weekends so they wouldn't get in the way.

I wasn't the only one whose life was dictated by a schedule. My mom drove me to the BMT Outpatient Clinic twice a week, fed me a nutritional snack every hour because I wasn't ready for three square meals a day, changed the dressings on my back each day in lieu of the nurses, and helped me prepare my TPN and other IVs every evening. Instead of coming home each night and watching the news, my dad assisted us any way he could. In the words of my mom, looking after me was "like caring for a newborn."

God gave us the grace to weather the storm of my first month home. We drew our strength from him, and we learned that life becomes less chaotic when you choose to be proactive. For instance, when the three of us assumed responsibility for operating the IV machines and preparing my IV medications, we eliminated the need for infusion specialists and reduced our contact with nurses. When we became the primary advocates for my health and well-being, the BMT staff at Georgetown became more accountable to us for their decisions about my care. We asked them every imaginable question about the course of my GVHD, the dosage of my medications, and the limits I needed to place on my activities. I'm convinced that doing so kept me out of the hospital. Finally, we discovered the value of rejoicing over small victories. When I passed my first semi-formed stool in early March, my mom raised her hands in triumph and exclaimed, "Your intestines are HEALING!!"

With the arrival of spring, my diarrhea became a fading memory and my TPN and IV medications were discontinued. By the last weekend of March, the wound on my back had completely healed, and I began enjoying hot showers for the first time in months. Although my blood levels remained low, I never required a transfusion. In just six short weeks, my prospects of returning to church, signing up for classes at school, and renewing my membership at the county rec center had moved within striking distance.

CHAPTER XXXI

Two-Thirds Full

I made remarkable progress my first two months home, but I never came close to feeling normal. Mild tissue damage at the site of my old incisions caused me pain whenever I took a deep breath, and the oral medications I took to control my GVHD (i.e., Cyclosporine, Imuran, and the steroid *Methylprednisolone*) made life insufferable for my GI tract. A moment never went by when I **didn't** feel nauseous. Worse yet, they compromised my fragile immune system, raised my blood pressure, interfered with my sleep, impeded my ability to regain lost muscle and bone mass, put me at risk for renal dysfunction, and caused fluid retention in my face and legs. I often felt as if I had 10 pound dumbbells strapped to my ankles.

When a GVHD-related skin rash flared up in late April, Dr. C., who monitored my care as an outpatient, changed my steroid prescription to the less toxic *Prednisone*.

"Rob, I want you to take this every other day at twice the dosage," he said. "Research has shown that it minimizes the side-effects without a drop-off in effectiveness."

My liver and kidneys benefited from the change, but I remained on the brink of nausea until mid-summer.

These nagging health problems seemed significant at the time, but I was doing far better than expected. Since my discharge, I'd eluded infections, avoided taking naps, and kept my GVHD in check. I lacked the stamina to engage in strenuous exercise, but I'm convinced that what little I did spurred on my recovery. I worked out every day on a treadmill, and as the days grew warmer, I took long walks around our neighborhood and in the area shopping malls.

My recovery gained momentum with the arrival of summer. That June, I resumed light weight lifting and using a stairclimber I purchased at the Sports Authority. Back to a normal eating schedule, I ate anything I wanted, except seafood. I had fish twice that summer, and both episodes culminated in severe vomiting and diarrhea. Suspecting that my marrow donor bequeathed a food allergy to me, I've avoided fish ever since.

By late-July, I'd gained 35 pounds, my blood and platelet counts had climbed to normal, my Hickman catheter had been removed, and I'd tapered off Prednisone. After months of limiting my social life to visits from friends, I began attending social gatherings outside the home and even saw *Forrest Gump* on the big screen. When Juanita and Butch came up for a visit the last weekend of July, Juanita was amazed at the progress I'd made since she and Betty visited me that previous December. "Why . . . Rob, you look fantastic!" she said, beaming.

"I feel pretty good too," I said, sheepishly.

"You know, it's only been five months since he left the hospital, and he looks like he's never been sick," my mom said.

"Uh-huh," Juanita said, nodding in agreement. "You look great, Sweetie."

Granted, I remained light years away from the strength and vigor I enjoyed before my relapse, but if you had asked me if my glass were half-full or half-empty, I would have answered "two-thirds full."

CHAPTER XXXII

Answering Back to the Potter

As the days of summer grew shorter and the smell of autumn approached, I brimmed with optimism. During the past two years, I'd weathered the shock of a cancer diagnosis, the devastation of a relapse, and the horror of a BMT. Each experience had brought me face to face with my mortality, each time I came out on top. It had been six months since I last passed through the double doors separating the Bone Marrow/Renal Transplant Unit from the rest of the world, and I was convinced my largest hurdles were behind me.

Two days before my family left for our annual vacation to the beach, however, I took a look at myself in the mirror and my heart sank.

I'm breaking out in a rash. GVHD . . . again. Will this ever end?

I had looked forward to this vacation for months. With the exception of the singles' retreat the previous October, it had been three years since I'd been to the beach. The last thing I needed was a recurrence of GVHD, even if it were just limited to my skin. Destined to remain photosensitive for the rest of my life as a result of the TBI, I'd been warned time and again about over-exposure to the sun. Not one to take my doctors' advice lightly, I wore long pants and 50 PFS sunscreen lotion whenever I ventured outside. This latest outbreak of GVHD made my skin all the more vulnerable, and I couldn't afford to let it go unnoticed, even if it meant canceling our trip.

The next day, I called Bonnie, who had recently become the BMT Outpatient Nurse Specialist, to alert her of my condition.

"A mild skin rash isn't necessarily a bad thing because you need some chronic GVHD to protect you from relapse," Bonnie assured me. "Is the GVHD confined to your skin?"

"Yes," I replied. "Otherwise, I'm fine. Dr. C. recently said my liver is 'perfect.'"

"Well, Rob, I would proceed with the vacation plans and make an appointment to come in for a visit your first Monday back in town," she said.

"Should I adjust my medication?" I asked.

"Not just yet," she answered. "We want to see if you can ride this rash out and force your new marrow to adjust." However, to be on the safe side, Dr. C. said he wants you to call him mid-week to update him on your condition."

"Okay," I said. "See you in two weeks."

Bonnie's advice was sound. During tapers of anti-rejection medications, many BMT patients reach a threshold they can't go below without an outbreak of GVHD. When this happens, patients experience an adjustment phase lasting anywhere from a few days to several months. Common symptoms during this time include dry eyes, itching skin, heartburn, greater susceptibility to infections, mild renal dysfunction, and sinus congestion.

Riding these phases out is unpleasant, but necessary. Before the donated marrow can accept the recipient's body, its T-cells must be activated and given the chance to adjust to their new home.[1] Increasing the medication at the first sign of chronic GVHD can sometimes be counter-productive because it delays the maturing of

---

[1] The T-Cells belong to the class of white cells known as the lymphocytes. Often referred to as "killer cells," they help other cells seek out and eradicate foreign proteins, form a natural defense against the growth and proliferation of cancer cells, and stimulate immune responses, such as allergic reactions and graft rejection. *The Signet Mosby Medical Encyclopedia*, Rev. ed. (New York: Penguin Books USA Inc., 1996), 481, 743.

the immune system.

Things were different in my case. When I tapered off Prednisone in late July, I never imagined that there might be a 2-3 week delay between a drop below my threshold and the first signs of GVHD. This GVHD outbreak began the third week of August, and more than likely, I'd exceeded my tolerance weeks earlier. When I returned home from the beach, I was covered head-to-toe with my worst skin rash in six months.

Needless to say, our trip to the beach wasn't all I hoped it would be when I dreamed about it months earlier in the hospital. I imagined myself running on the beach or swimming in the warm Atlantic without a care in the world. When I reached the anticipated event, I lacked the leg strength to run on the beach, avoided swimming in the ocean for fear of catching an infection, and stayed out of the sun in peak hours because of my skin condition. As for my parents, they were so concerned with monitoring my health that neither of them enjoyed themselves. That said, just walking on the beach and breathing the warm, salty air had its own rewards.

When I saw Dr. C. the following week, it was too late for a minor adjustment of my meds. Of primary importance now was getting the GVHD under control before it spread to my liver or intestines. Confident I would taper down to a good maintenance level within a matter of weeks, I wasn't too disappointed when he put me on 80 mg. of Prednisone every other day.

Several days passed without improvement, and the optimistic outlook that had sustained me for so long went out of me like the air of a balloon.

All this time I've projected my recovery in terms of weeks and months. What if I have to start thinking in terms of years? Please, God . . . I don't need this.

"Mom!" I shouted.

"What is it?" she asked.

"The rash," I answered. "Look! It's been a week since Dr. C. put me back on Prednisone, and it hasn't done squat. How long am I going to have to put up with GVHD? How long?!"

"Rob, I don't know how long this is going to take," she said, sighing. "But, you know, God's going to do this in his timing, and we just have to accept it."

"I can tell right now that I'm not coming off these drugs anytime soon," I said.

"I don't know what to tell you, Rob," she said.

"Are you saying I might be immunosuppressed for the next three years?" I asked, becoming more agitated.

"You might," my dad said, joining the conversation.

"What about my returning to church or school?" I asked.

"Rob, don't shoot the messenger," my dad said. "If complaining ever solved anything, we'd call everyone and hold a joint complaining session. It doesn't do any good, so why do it?"

"Because I want to!" I countered.

All the disappointment, frustration, and anger that I'd buried since my relapse exploded to the surface, and I wanted to lash out at everyone. For the next month, I was anything but the "courageous cancer survivor who is an inspiration to all who know him." Sometimes I became so hostile that my dad would leave the room in disgust. He couldn't understand how someone who had received so much could now be so ungrateful. I didn't understand it myself.

One night, I woke up feeling a white-hot anger that was so intense, I started punching my pillow with my fist. When I heard my mom cleaning up in the kitchen, I decided to go downstairs and make her life miserable as well. She had a higher tolerance for my behavior than my dad, understanding that the steroids probably intensified my mood swings. However, she drew the line when I started throwing dishes, causing slivers of glass to fly in all directions.

"Rob! Get ahold of yourself!" she demanded. "You're not the only one suffering here," she said, tears streaming down her face.

"Well, I've lived with this crap for a year, and I'm sick and tired of it!" I huffed.

"Guess who's also sick of it —" my mom began.

"Yeah, yeah, I know," I said, interrupting her. "But you're not the patient. I AM!!!"

"Rob, we know what you've gone through. WE WENT THROUGH IT WITH YOU!!" she shouted. "Ever since your back flared up, I've been confused and angry too," she continued. "But I just know that God is going to heal you and that he has a reason for allowing this to happen."

"Oh, come on!" I scoffed. "I had enough GVHD to cure my

leukemia before I left the hospital!"

"You don't know that for certain," she said.

"I'll bet God's just doing this to teach me patience," I said. "Well, guess what? I'm sick of him 'teaching' me something. If this is life after a BMT then I don't want it!"

"Rob, how can you say that?" she asked. "You're ALIVE! You should be thankful."

"Well, I'm not," I replied. "He hasn't done enough. YOU HEAR ME?! IT'S NOT ENOUGH!!!" I shouted at the top of my lungs, believing that if I screamed loud enough it might hurt God's feelings all the more. And I wanted to hurt him. I felt like cursing him.

I had a deep-seated animosity toward God over the issue of timing. Reconciling his sense of timing with mine had been my number one struggle since my diagnosis, and this issue came to a head as a result of this latest skin rash. I knew the quality of my post-leukemia health pivoted on the goal of becoming free of GVHD. It's only by the grace of God that I didn't know just how long it would take me to reach that goal. My rash would take several months to clear up, and even that might not have happened if Georgetown hadn't added the drug *Plaquenil* to my regimen in mid-October.

Before my BMT, I assumed my recovery would last 6-12 months. Long before my discharge, I made a mental list of everything I planned to accomplish during my first three years post-transplant: bench press my body weight by Summer '95, run a 10K race before my 28th birthday, and graduate from Marymount with a second Masters degree in May '97. Finding a job, moving out on my own, and getting this book published would follow shortly thereafter. Now I couldn't even return to church.

I never counted on chronic GVHD becoming such a problem. The more persistent the GVHD, the longer the stay on my medications and the longer my immune system remained compromised. For the unrelated BMT survivor, it can take well over a year before one can return to public life without the constraints of a surgical mask. That October, I asked Dr. R., who had replaced Dr. C. as my primary care physician, if I still needed to wear a mask. I hated wearing one in public. It was embarrassing.

"At this point in your recovery, you don't need one outdoors as

long as you avoid crowds and stay away from areas like construction sites," she replied.

"I haven't worn a mask outdoors since June," I said. "I know I
still need to wear it in hospitals, but what about shopping malls,
restaurants, and other indoor public places?"

"Avoid malls and restaurants at peak hours," she said. "If you go
there during times when they're not so busy, that's fine, but you still
ought to wear a mask."

"How long until I no longer need to wear one?" I asked.

"We'd like to get you off the steroids first," she said.

That's what I thought. This really sucks!

When I composed my first draft of this chapter on Thanksgiving
Day '94, I still wore a mask in all public indoor places and I had yet
to return to church.

The social isolation was even worse than the prospect of delaying
my fitness or career goals. Much worse. During my first year out of
the hospital, my social life was primarily limited to my home. My
brother David came over for lunch once or twice a week, and I
hosted a small bible study with a few of my friends from church on
Thursday nights. However, my first interaction with a large group
of people outside of my house and **without** a mask was a birthday
party for my friend Lori in late September.

My frustration with God went beyond the issue of time. Since my
diagnosis, I'd always assumed my healing would be "total and
complete," just as Ruth and Dad's words of knowledge had stated.[2]
Now I wondered if those words should be taken at face value.

*Perhaps God's definition of a total and complete healing is
different from mine.*

I refused to accept any variation of "quality of life" that didn't
encompass a total and complete recovery from the BMT.

*God, your definition of 'total and complete' better mean what I
want it to mean. A cure for my leukemia isn't enough if it means
having to live with life-long side-effects from the BMT. Do you hear
me God? That's not good enough!*

The mature perspective would have been for me to be thankful I

---

[2] See Chapter VIII.

was alive. In fact, when people told me that, I wanted to rip their heads off. I know they were trying to be helpful, but all they did was rub salt in my wounds. It's easy for people to say, "Just be thankful it's not worse" when they're healthy and haven't experienced medical problems that keep them from doing the things most of us take for granted.

Frankly, I didn't want to take the mature path. I loved God, but lashing out in anger toward him had an emotional pay-off. I had no right to demand anything from him, but I relished the idea of doing so. I found shaking my fist in the face of someone I couldn't beat intoxicating. It gave me the same fiendish joy I experienced as a child whenever I shouted insults at the neighborhood bully. I may have been acting like a fool, but I felt powerful.

Deep down, I knew God had a purpose for this latest setback and that one day, I might thank him. I also knew that if his promise of a "total and complete" healing didn't mean a return to full health in this lifetime, he'd give me the grace to accept it. Being human, my view was limited. I just wanted to be normal again.

My friend Lisa anticipated the emotional struggle I'd have in reconciling God's purposes with my own. Three months before this latest recurrence of GVHD, she sent me a letter urging me to resist setting time constraints on my recovery. She said that from her own observation and experience, the most complete and long-lasting recoveries are those which take time. She told me that the major issue for me in the coming months would be learning to recognize that when I'm healed isn't as important as the fact that I **will** be restored to health at a time set by God, not me.

I didn't give Lisa's letter much credence when I first received it because she wasn't telling me what I wanted to hear. When I re-read her letter in September, however, I was amazed at the timeliness of her advice. My mom re-read her letter as well, and she reminded me of what Lisa told me one afternoon when she visited me at the hospital.

"I know she visited me, but I was strung out on pain medications at the time," I recalled. "I don't remember what she said."

"Well, it certainly brightened your outlook that day," my mom replied. "Lisa said, 'The time you've spent fighting your illness hasn't been wasted. From God's standpoint, your life is right on schedule. You might be tempted to ask him why he's allowed this to happen, but just remember that he has a purpose for it. You can trust him.'"

In the ensuing months since my mom reminded me of Lisa's visit, I drew strength and encouragement from those words. They were simple, but profound: God is not limited by time or space. In his economy, I'd lose time only if I wasted it feeling sorry for myself.

CHAPTER XXXIII

The Pain of Dependence

Later that fall, I read *Finding God,* by Larry Crabb, Jr. , a respected Christian Psychologist and writer. In this penetrating and somewhat controversial book, Crabb addresses issues that have vexed people of faith ever since Adam and Eve were kicked out of Eden. Among these are affirming God's justice when life is unfair, experiencing God's grace in the midst of suffering, and the meaning of true contentment.

Having viewed the book's companion video series in Sunday School months earlier, April warned me that I might find Crabb's message "disturbing." Some of our peers had found it downright offensive! Giving a counselor that kind of warning is like telling a toddler there are cookies in the pantry. I delved right in and received insights that reframed my struggles with God better than any preacher could have done from the pulpit.

The cry of the human heart is intimacy with God. Above all else, it's this drive for a relationship with our Creator that separates us from the animal kingdom. According to Crabb, the barrier that keeps us from experiencing this intimacy with God and by extension, one another, is our obsession with self-gratification.[1]

---

[1] Larry Crabb, *Finding God* (Grand Rapids, MI: Zondervan Publishing House, 1993) 15-20.

We humans prefer life to be painless, free of hassles, and fulfilling. When our pursuit of this state of bliss eclipses our hunger for God, our noblest desires become so twisted and distorted that their final result is anything but what God intended. Who among us hasn't exchanged love for lust, used generosity as a bribe, or presented a facade of humility to further our own interests? If we're honest, we'd have to admit that even when we do seek God on a personal level, we're often motivated by selfishness.

I've been a Christian for two decades, and I'm amazed at how often I rebel against God on the one hand and demand he fulfill my desires on the other. Sometimes, I don't even recognize this until my desires are frustrated and I question his wisdom and goodness. As a result of reading Crabb's book, I realized that I hadn't changed much since my relapse. The gulf between the beliefs I espoused and the beliefs I lived by remained. I didn't trust God. Not from the depths of my heart.

During my stay in the hospital, trusting God was easy because I had no hope of surviving without him. Six months after my discharge, I felt it was safe for him to let go of the reigns so I could resume control of my life. I was eating a balanced diet, working out, getting plenty of rest, and committed to a full recovery. No matter what I did, however, I was powerless against GVHD. Only God could bring my marrow and my body into unity, and he moved at a snail's pace.

Another thing I learned from reading Crabb's book was how I valued my independence more than God's love. I had lived that way for years, and the BMT didn't change that at all. During those long months in the hospital, I vowed I'd never again become so dependent that nurses would have to clean me up after I vomited or defecated on myself. As vulnerable as I felt when I was finally allowed to return home, I regarded my ordeal in the same way Mr. Mayagi, in *The Karate Kid*, viewed catching a fly with chopsticks. When Daniel (Ralph Macchio) inquired about this bizarre behavior, Mayagi (Pat Morita) replied, "Man who catch fly with chopsticks accomplish anything."

After what I'd experienced, I assumed my recovery would be a snap. When I discovered that I still needed to depend on God months later, it drove me crazy. I wanted him to get out of the way so I could take charge.

If there had been a nutritional plan that guaranteed a return to full health, I would have followed it. If scripture memorization had been the key, I would have memorized the entire Bible. Truth is, I had stopped reading through those scriptures I meditated on in the hospital months earlier because I assumed the worst was behind me. They gave me no guarantees of immediate healing, so I figured, *Why bother?* I wanted a formula, and there was none to be found.

Chapter XXXIV

The Big Picture

As the days grew shorter and winter approached, I gradually became sick of fighting with God because I knew it wouldn't make the GVHD go away any sooner. Furthermore, I was making the lives of everyone around me miserable including my own. Although every bone in my body recoiled at the prospect of fighting GVHD indefinitely, I knew that submitting my will to the Potter's higher wisdom was the only solution available.

God, I don't understand why you've allowed this setback to happen. I'm taking more medication now that I was last April. But you have said in your Word that you will cause all things to work out for the good of those who love you. Help me to learn everything you want to teach me through this, Lord, and give me the grace to accept your timing as superior to mine. And forgive me for acting so ungrateful. In reality, I'm actually progressing faster than many would have predicted. Please help me to remember that.

I prayed those words for months. Submitting your will to God is a process, not a one-time decision. However, as a result of humbling myself before him, I was finally able to see the big picture. And I saw that my glass was still two-thirds full.

For example, since early September, my bouts with nausea had become far less frequent, and the fluid retention in my legs and ankles had virtually disappeared. This second development, a sign that my kidneys were returning to normal, puzzled everyone because it was the opposite of what we expected when I went back on Prednisone. Dr. R. couldn't explain it. However, blood tests later confirmed that my kidneys were in wonderful shape.

I had no idea how well my recovery had progressed until I attended the Annual Georgetown BMT Reunion in late October. It had been a mere eight months since I'd left the hospital, and I looked as healthy as anyone there, including patients who had been cancer-free for years. Witnessing this firsthand gave my attitude a dramatic boost.

The nurses who attended the reunion expressed amazement at how well I looked. One of them didn't even recognize me until I identified myself. Many of my fellow BMT patients from the previous year were less fortunate. Several died while I was an inpatient, and three others whom I had known personally died within a year of my leaving the hospital.

The first of these three patients, Joel, was my age and a professing Christian. Diagnosed with Acute Lymphatic Leukemia (ALL) in 1987, he'd been through six relapses. Although he finally underwent a BMT in 1992, courtesy of his twin brother, it was too little, too late. The weekend prior to my discharge, he was back for another. A month later, he died in the ICU.

I have to give Joel credit. Hard of hearing and in need of a cane to walk, both caused by years of radiation, he fought for his life until the very end. His odds of surviving the procedure a second time, let alone being cured of his disease, were slim. Even if he had been cured, his physical health and strength would never have returned to the level he enjoyed before his disease. Furthermore, whereas I had family, friends, and entire churches behind me, Joel had only his twin brother for support. His parents were deceased.

The next patient, Mark, was admitted to the BMT unit in late January '94. A father of two young children, his prognosis was far worse than mine. In a state of resistant relapse, he sought a BMT in a last ditch effort to put his leukemia into remission. His prospects for a cure were remote.

Unlike Joel, Mark had a good support system. His sister was his donor, and his wife, an elementary schoolteacher, was as kind a person as you will find. During her visits to the hospital, she sometimes dropped by to see me as well. One evening, she even gave me a stack of red hearts made from construction paper so I could decorate my walls for Valentine's Day.

Mark breezed through his transplant. Although my transplant was three months earlier, he was discharged two weeks after me and looked far better. I envied him because he could eat anything he wanted, and I was happy just keeping plain yogurt down without upchucking.

When I saw him the following June, our situations were reversed. His GVHD had kicked in big-time. Not only had he lost weight, but his hair hadn't grown back yet. I did my best to cheer him up by saying his GVHD might be a blessing in disguise, but sadly, the afternoon I saw him may have been his last as an outpatient. I found out two years later that he died of a relapse that summer.

The final patient, Tren, was a young Vietnamese woman who immigrated to the United States after the fall of Saigon. Like Mark, she sailed through her treatment with no complications. Several months later, however, she experienced a fierce outbreak of GVHD. When I saw her at the BMT Reunion, she was taking three time my dosage of Prednisone, her Cyclosporine prescription was so high that her hands trembled, and she complained that her skin "itched like crazy." Her energy paled in comparison to mine, and she told me she often became depressed over how she looked and felt.

I felt a real connection to Tren, probably because she and I were the same age and the only unrelated BMT patients at Georgetown that previous winter. She was kind, engaging, and thoughtful. Because she was still in isolation when I was discharged, I didn't meet her until later that spring. However, she often asked about me, knowing I'd had a rough time of it.

The BMT Reunion was the third and last time I saw her. She told me she wanted to stay in touch and invite me over for dinner with her and her boyfriend sometime in the near future. Shortly thereafter, she died of a fungal infection.

The lives of Joel, Mark, and Tren bear witness to the fact that NOBODY breezes through cancer, regardless of their strength, youth, or vitality. Although I resented having to rely on my parents and doctors, I had all the reason in the world to celebrate that November when several of my friends threw me a surprise party for my 27th birthday.

Chapter XXXV

Return to the Land of the Living

The week after Thanksgiving, Dr. R. gave me the green light to return to public life without a face mask. When the prospect of no longer sticking out finally materialized, the rush of freedom I felt rivaled the first time I drove my dad's '73 Super Beetle by myself.

"Rob, you be careful," my mom cautioned. "It's flu season, and I'm not wild about you going places without a mask. I know what Dr. R. said, but I think you should move slow." Then she added, "Besides, why do you care what people think when they see you wearing a mask?"

"Mom, people usually don't say anything, but I hate drawing attention to myself," I said.

Truth is, I felt naked the first month I went places without a mask. I saw everything as a source of infection from doorknobs and salad bars to Santa Claus himself. A cough or sneeze from across the room made me paranoid. I didn't eat food from the buffet unless the restaurant had a microwave, I washed the tops of soda cans before drinking, and I used a napkin to take the cap off a bottle of ketchup. Unsure of how much protection my flu shot provided me, I avoided children and prayed for protection whenever I walked onto a crowded elevator.

I finally returned to Sunday School in early December. Since my leukemia diagnosis, the singles' group at CFC had been my primary social, as well as spiritual, outlet. Outside of my volunteer work in Spring '93, I hadn't worked since Summer '91. I didn't have a network of co-workers to hang out with, and my old high school friends had moved on with their lives years earlier. This group was it. They were the ones I thought about during those long months in virtual isolation.

The morning I walked into our classroom, several of my peers grew wide-eyed and rushed to greet me with a warm hug. When they told me how wonderful I looked, they were celebrating a triumph in which they all had a part. They had prayed for me, supported me, and visited me during the loneliest times of my exile in the hospital. For some of them, this was the first time they saw the fruit of their labor. In commemoration of the occasion, one of them wrote out in big letters on the chalkboard: ROB IS BACK!!

Fourteen months had passed since the singles' group laid their hands on me and prayed for God's protection and healing. So much had happened since then, both in their lives and mine. Kelley left for Michigan the day after I went into the hospital, and his replacement was hired the following February. Although Pastor Wayne had paid a visit to my home in late June, I didn't know what to expect from him or the group.

Several of my friends had married. During my year-long hiatus from the group, I turned down six wedding invitations because of my medical condition. Two weeks before Dr. Z. informed me of my relapse, my friend Rob asked me to serve as an usher in his wedding that coming October. Although he found someone else to fill my place, he left the door open for me to be part of the wedding party if my health permitted. As fate had it, I was admitted for my BMT six days prior to his wedding.

Soon after I came home from the hospital, our church finalized the purchase of our present location in Ashburn, VA. In the wake of our impending move to Loudoun County, many of my closest friends had left or were intending to leave CFC for houses of worship closer to home. Despite the initial joy of the moment, reintegrating myself back into church life wouldn't be as easy as I first anticipated. Things had changed.

That January, I returned to Marymount University. Prior to my diagnosis, I took college life for granted. As I watched nervous underclassmen scurry from class to class and listened to student athletes bond together at a nearby practice field, it made me come alive. I felt like I was making something of myself; pursuing a goal. I hadn't known that feeling since May '93.

When I signed up for "Theories of Counseling," the class I dropped at the time of my relapse, I wasn't even sure my professor would remember me. I was a nondegree matriculate, and it had been 18 months since Dr. B. had scolded me for eating pizza during his lecture. Nevertheless, that first night, he asked, "Can you stick around for a moment, Robert?"

"Sure," I said.

As the last of the students filtered out of the room, he broke into a wide grin, extended his hand, and asked, "So, how have you been?"

"Well, I'm doing pretty well," I replied, smiling. "They found a marrow donor in England who matched me perfectly, including DNA and bloodtype, and I had a BMT in October '93."

"That's great, Robert," he said. "I remember when you had to drop my class several semesters ago, and I was wondering how you've been. When I saw your name on the roll sheet I felt like shouting. So how's your health now?"

"I had a pretty rough time of it in the hospital, particularly with Graft vs. Host Disease [GVHD], a temporary condition in which the cells of my new marrow tried to attack my body as a foreign entity," I explained. "It's still somewhat of a problem, but my doctors have told me it's a good thing in the long-run because it's probably killed off any leukemia cells that were left after the radiation and chemotherapy."

"Really? That's interesting," he said.

"Yeah, they told me while I was still in the hospital that I had a good chance of being cured of my disease," I said. "We're keeping the GVHD under control with a number of medications, but I still have some mild symptoms like itchy skin, dry eyes, and a suppressed immune system. Two months ago, I wasn't sure whether I'd even be able to return to school this semester."

"Well, I'm glad you're back," he said.

"Me too," I replied. "Until recently, I avoided crowds and wore a surgical mask whenever I went to public places like shopping malls, churches, or hospitals."

"I can't imagine what that's like. I'll bet you really feel proud of yourself," he said.

"Well, you know, I have to give God the credit for my healing, along with the care of excellent doctors," I answered.

I didn't want to push my Christian faith on him, but I couldn't help sharing what God had done in my life and how several churches across the country had prayed for me. I don't know what impression it made on him, but he seemed impressed, especially when I told him how committed my parents and family had been to me.

"Thank God, for parents," he said. "Thank God for parents."

We talked for a little while longer about my plans of becoming a licensed therapist and writing a book about my experience. When we parted company, he said, "It's made my day seeing you."

His reaction was typical of people who have discovered that I went through a BMT. Before the transplant, I assumed I had a boring testimony about my Christian experience. I came to Christ in my 3rd grade Sunday School class, and I'd never done anything that would hit the cover of *Newsweek*. Now I was seeing firsthand how my cancer experience could open doors for me to witness about God's love and healing power in ways I never would have envisioned. With that in mind, my frustrations just faded into the background and I caught a brighter glimpse of what it means to see life from God's perspective instead of my own.

Chapter XXXVI

By Leaps, Bounds and a Stumble

During the spring of '95, I tapered my dosage of Prednisone down to 10 mg. every other day, and my energy level skyrocketed. Body image and physical stamina have been intertwined with my self-concept for years, but I never realized how important my appearance was to me until after the BMT. As my health improved, so did my looks and self-esteem. When I looked in the mirror, I no longer saw a face swollen twice its normal size or the fragile physique of a cancer patient. The only reminder of how things had changed was my hair.

For most of my life, my wavy brown hair was my pride and joy. Outside of my blue eyes, women gave me more compliments on my hair than any other physical characteristic. Before my BMT, Radiation Medicine warned me that some TBI candidates suffer permanent hair loss. Hearing those words struck at my sense of personhood far more than learning I might end up sterile. I became indignant at the suggestion, so much so that my dad said, "Well, you know, God might allow that to teach you a lesson. You can't dictate to God what side-effects he can or can't allow as a result of your treatment. If I were bald, but cured of my leukemia, I'd consider it a good pay-off. You're being vain."

I am vain at times. Several years ago, I made a crack about my friend John's lack of hair, and he replied, "Rob, you'll live to regret that statement." Well, guess what? Thanks to the cumulative effects of TBI and chronic GVHD, my hair has never regained its former glory, and I gets thinner every year. I stopped carrying a comb six years ago, and most people now consider me bald.

I couldn't afford Rogaine, but I did everything else to improve my appearance. In addition to exercise, I ate a balanced diet, reduced my intake of junk food, and I used my juicer every night. The steroids never blew me up beyond proportion, but when I began working out in November, I was 15-20 pounds overweight. By July, I weighed a svelte 172, just seven pounds heavier than my graduating weight at ORU. I wasn't buff, but I looked good, especially for someone who had come back from the brink of death. Because I regained all the strength I lost after my relapse, I had no doubt I would be as good as new in no time at all.

By mid-July, I was convinced that I was 85 percent back to normal. I was almost off Cyclosporine, and I had seen no signs of GVHD. As I looked forward to our first joint vacation to the beach with my mom's family in 13 years, my optimism knew no bounds.

Things went so well that I grew lax in caring for my health. I went to every social event that came my way, forgetting that a BMT survivor's body often betrays him. A week before we were scheduled to leave for the beach, I came down with a respiratory infection, throwing our plans in jeopardy.

Three days on antibiotics changed nothing. That Wednesday evening I stayed up all night long coughing up so much yellow mucus that I feared I might be getting bronchitis. Resigning myself to the probability of a cancelled vacation, I scheduled an appointment with Dr. R. the next day.

"Robert," Dr. R. began, "I'm glad you came in now because we need to take an X-ray of your sinuses and a CAT scan of your head and lungs before the radiologists go home for the evening."

"Why do I need a CAT scan?" I asked.

"With BMT patients on immunosuppressants, problems such as yours can be symptoms of a serious condition," she replied. "CAT scans are better than X-rays for ruling out such possibilities."

"Can fungal infections be manifested in the sinuses?" I asked.

"Yes, but I really don't think you have one," she assured me. "More than likely it's just sinusitis, but since you're leaving for the beach this weekend, I want to be on the safe side."

"So, it's alright for us to go to the beach, even with this infection?" I asked.

"The beach is the best place for you to be right now because of the humid, salty air," she answered. "While you're there, I want you to call Bonnie on Monday or Tuesday to let us know how you're doing."

The CAT scan indicated nothing more than sinusitis, but my parents harbored their doubts about going to the beach. I knew they might be right, but I had been looking forward to this vacation for months. Most of my cousins would be there for at least part of the week, one of whom I hadn't seen since my graduation from ORU. Besides, I had a sinus infection before I went on the Singles' retreat to Virginia Beach in October '93, and the salty air did wonders for me.

I still felt sick the morning we left for the beach, but I'd already made up my mind. Praying about it was a formality to absolve myself from feeling guilty. I might as well have just said, "God, if this isn't your will, big deal! I'm going anyway.

The trip to the beach did more harm than good. The weather was hot and sticky; the very conditions residents around the Capital Beltway hope to escape when they leave for the beach. Our accommodations were excellent, but going in and out of an air-conditioned beach house in that kind of weather just exacerbated my problems. My cough became worse, so much so that I could no longer lay down without coughing. On the third night there, my aunt Betty, who's had chronic asthma and bronchitis for years, said, "That cough's gone into your chest."

"You think so?" I asked.

"I would know that sound as well as anyone," she replied.

"Rob, how do you feel right now?" My mother asked.

"Well, I was feeling pretty good earlier today, but my cough's gotten worse," I admitted.

We took my temperature, which came out normal, and then my mother asked, "Do you think you should call Dr. R.?"

"Probably," I replied. I was seven hours away from Georgetown hospital, and I feared my cough might degenerate into pneumonia. The thought of being admitted to the hospital for a lower respiratory infection conjured up unpleasant memories of IVs, chest tubes, and exploratory surgery. I wanted to avoid that as much as possible, so I called Dr. R. long-distance to tell her I was coming home the next day.

"Well, I'm sorry to hear that," Dr. R. said. "Are you still taking *Ceftin*?"

"Yes," I said.

"Increase your dosage to three times a day," she instructed me. "Make sure you take *Robitussin* every six hours, drink lots of fluids, and call my office as soon as you get home. I'll arrange for you to see an ear, nose and throat specialist later this week."

Our vacation was cut short, but to be honest, it wasn't really a vacation. I enjoyed seeing my relatives, but I couldn't kick back and relax because of my health problems. As for my parents, this was the second year in a row that their vacation to the beach was more stressful than staying home. They were so concerned with my health and the cleanliness of our living conditions that neither of them had time to unwind.

The events of the past week were a reality check. I had a way to go before I was back to normal. That respiratory infection was only the beginning.

Chapter XXXVII

A Season of Setbacks

===

Our aborted trip to the beach marked the beginning of a long impasse in my recovery. Chronic sinus troubles plagued me for months. My summer was all but ruined as backyard barbecues, outings to the lake, and excursions to the movies became more trouble than they were worth. Every time I stepped outside, I started coughing.

My sinuses had bothered me off and on since my BMT, but drinking plenty of fluids and using nasal sprays usually kept the problems to a minimum. Now my life resembled the experiences of people suffering from media-hyped conditions such as "multichemical sensitivity" and "sick building syndrome." Everything from ceiling fans to the smell of household bleach affected me, and conventional treatment provided modest relief at best. As the days grew colder, one or both of my parents began to accompany me to the hospital or school so they could let me out at the front of the building to minimize my risk of getting sick. For the next year, I missed church more often than not because going just made things worse.

One afternoon, I asked Dr. R. why I continued to experience such problems, and she suggested they might be the growing pains of my new immune system. "Your donor's marrow probably has more histamine receptors than yours did," she said. "Remember, your immune system is now two years old, and you're on less medications than you were last year. Perhaps it's starting to react to the surrounding environment."

"You know, I've suspected that my donor might have more airborne allergies or be more sensitive to drafts than I am because I never experienced these problems before my transplant," I said. "Did the Cyclosporine mask these problems a year ago?"

"That's very possible," she replied. "In a few years, you might want to move further south if the cold air and extreme changes between the seasons continue to affect you."

My problems didn't end with my sinuses. When I came off Cyclosporine for good in late August, I had to double my steroid dosage to counteract GVHD. Unable to taper the Prednisone down to it's previous level the following April, its effect on my joints was debilitating. Chronic joint pain in my elbows, ankles, knees. and right shoulder precluded me from lifting weights or using the stairclimber without risk of injury.

Working out had been my favorite pastime for months. You could probably say I'd become addicted to it. I loved working out because it relieved stress and prolonged the illusion that I was normal. Not being able to lift weights, run, or romp on the stairclimber for so long took its toll. I gained 20 pounds over the next four months, and I brimmed with jealousy every time I saw a Bally's Total Fitness commercial on TV. I knew I might never look as good as the ideal depicted on my TV screen, but I yearned for the opportunity to aspire to that goal. By mid-December, I had been reduced to seeing a physical therapist every two weeks, icing my joints several times a day, and petitioning Marymount University for a handicap parking sticker. I dreaded what might happen if things didn't turn around soon.

What's next, God? A cane or wheelchair?

As Winter '96 approached, I feared that more setbacks lurked just around the corner. My parents and I did everything in our power to avoid a confrontation with the flu. We decided not to spend Christmas with my mom's family in North Carolina, and I avoided going to church during January and February, even though it had become my only opportunity for social contact outside of school. In spite of these efforts, our worst fears were realized in late February. The flu knocked me flat on my back with a deep chest cough, no appetite, joints that ached to the point that I could hardly walk, and a temperature of 102.5 Fahrenheit. At Dr. R.'s insistence, I checked into the hospital on a Tuesday afternoon, and I returned home the following Sunday.

I'd managed to avoid being admitted to the hospital for exactly two years to the day. When I left the hospital in February '94, I never dreamed that an admittance to the hospital for five days of IV antibiotics at this point in my recovery would still be a possibility. Now it had happened, and I resented God.

Why don't you just heal me so I don't have to check with doctors or think about my health every time I make a decision? Why, God?

I longed for the days when I revelled in the illusion of being in charge of my own health. On the rare occasions when I became ill as a college student, I popped in at the local doctor's office, stated my complaints, and requested a prescription. CAT scans, trips to the hospital, and IVs never crossed my radar screen. Now ailments I once considered insignificant, including the flu, had become major events that affected everyone in my sphere of influence.

If a family therapist or social worker had been asked to describe my family during this time, he or she would have labeled us as "enmeshed" or "codependent." And with good reason. Everything revolved around my medical condition. None of us made a decision without evaluating its effect on my health. I believe David and Brenda often felt pushed aside because these issues dominated the conversations at our family get-togethers. I bore as much guilt as my parents, and we all had to make an effort to keep our discussions from centering around me.

They don't give instruction manuals to families when a member is diagnosed with cancer. We'd just spent the past three years muddling through an experience that can split loving families apart, and by the grace of God, we'd remained together. If we became codependent along the way, it was a small price to pay. During the winter of '96, however, I felt trapped.

I felt trapped, not only because I had to depend upon parents and doctors, but also because my social life floundered. Although due in part to my medical condition, our church's move to Loudoun County also played a role. My closest friends were now either married or attending other churches. As a result, it didn't take long for me to start feeling isolated and lonely.

My peers at church weren't to blame for any of this. Many of them went out of their way to make me feel like I still belonged to their group. However, my health status precluded me from committing to most of the social events or service projects sponsored by the singles' ministry. I found it difficult to establish new relationships, and as a result, I felt like I was part of an organization as opposed to a community.

This sense of disconnectedness went beyond the church. I felt that way with everyone. It wasn't until I came across an article in *Coping* (a magazine for cancer survivors and their families) a year later that I was able to put these feelings into words.[1] The authors' experiences were so similar to mine that I could have written it myself. Their main point was that most cancer survivors feel socially "out of sync" when they return to public life. Accustomed to the closeness, vulnerability, and openness they experienced with family and friends during treatment, they expect it to continue beyond the crisis. When they reemerge into the real world, they become disappointed and confused because everyone else has moved on and expects them to do the same.[2]

When I returned to public life in December '94, I promised myself and God that I wouldn't milk my leukemia experience to receive attention from others. I'm ashamed to admit that although I said I wanted to be treated as a regular guy and not a leukemia survivor, I felt hurt when the novelty of my BMT wore off and people no longer treated me as if I were special.

My sense of social disconnectedness went far deeper than my narcissistic longings for affirmation. Truth is, my desire to be treated as normal was unrealistic because I wasn't normal. My health habits and lifestyle no longer resembled those of the average person. Friends and extended family tried to accommodate me, but they sometimes couldn't understand why someone who looks healthy turns down a part-time job with flexible hours, campouts in

---

[1] Glenna Halvorson-Boyd and Lisa K. Hunter. "Cancer Changes Our Lives — and Our Relationships." *Coping* May/June 1997: 68.
[2] Ibid.

the Shenandoah, weekend retreats in Pennsylvania, and all-you-can-eat buffets for medical reasons. They didn't know what I expected of them, and with good reason: Neither did I.

My social life might have improved if I'd shown initiative. Since I couldn't go out as often as the average person, I assumed people would grow bored with me. I planned nothing, called no one, and sunk into loneliness and isolation.

Sometimes, God has to break you before he can mold you. If my recovery had stayed on track, I would have taken life for granted once again. As a loving potter, God knows what it takes to fashion me into a person who instinctively praises him even when circumstances tempt me to do otherwise. I'm not there yet, so the process continues.

Chapter XXXVIII

A Season of Discontent

The setbacks of Winter '96 forced me to take life at a slower pace. I looked healthy, but as I'd just learned, common conditions like the flu could still become major league crises. Upon my discharge from Georgetown the first week of March, I dropped a class I was scheduled to begin later that month and decided to postpone my graduation plans for a year.

I dreaded situations where I had to make my health concerns an issue because I was afraid others would think I was using my medical condition to receive preferential treatment. I found nothing more anxiety-provoking than asking a group of people in a stuffy room to turn down a fan because it irritated my sinuses. Most of the time, I suffered in silence.

With the arrival of summer, my knees deteriorated to the point I couldn't exercise at all. Forced to limit my use of the stairs, I relied on my parents to be my hands and feet. If I were studying upstairs and wanted a snack, my mom brought it to me. If my car needed to be washed and vacuumed, my dad did it for me. Here I was approaching the 3rd anniversary of my BMT, and our family revolved around me more than ever.

Depressed and frustrated, I stopped counting my blessings. I no longer marveled over how nurses who cared for me two years earlier now called me a miracle. My recovery was locked in a state of inertia, and I saw little reason to thank God for what he'd accomplished in my life.

I yearned for the life I enjoyed before the cancer. I missed the exhilaration of diving into the ocean to retrieve a frisbee, the satisfaction of moving the pin up a notch on a weight machine, and the embarrassment of blowing a coverage on the football field. What hurt most of all was my inability to do the mundane things I once took for granted, such as mowing the lawn, sprinting across campus to make a class on time, or helping a friend move into a new apartment. In all honesty, I've never longed for anything more than the chance to do these things once again.

That summer, my emotional state spiraled down to its lowest point since September '94. My social life became nonexistent. I withdrew from everyone, including my parents. Whenever my mother asked if I were depressed, I became defensive and insisted, "Mom, would you stop asking me that? I'm fine!"

A support group at my church entitled, "Experiencing God's Grace in the Midst of Chronic or Life-threatening Illness" became my saving grace that summer. If not for my participation in this group, who knows how deep I would have fallen! As a BMT survivor, I assumed my problems were unique; that I had a premium on physical suffering, a compromised immune system, and symptoms that raised more questions than answers.

Our group represented a cross-section of medical problems, some of which seemed more debilitating than mine. In spite of our differences in age, stage of life, and diagnosis, we struggled with the same feelings of anxiety, anger, and depression, and we wrestled with the same issues of reduced self-esteem, lost independence, financial insecurity, and social isolation. Although I co-founded and cofacilitated this group, its members helped me more than I helped them. Better yet, their stories convinced me that if given the chance, I wouldn't swap diagnoses with any of them.

Although the group started me on the process of dealing with my depression, discontent with life, and disillusion with God, Dr. R. provided the real trigger. She had been in charge of my care for the past two years and knew me well. The moment she saw me when I came in for my August appointment, she noticed I was no longer the vibrant, cheerful, optimistic patient she'd raved about since my discharge from the hospital.

"Robert, why so serious?" she exclaimed. "This is not the Robert I know."

"What do you mean?" I asked.

"Well, you're usually so upbeat!" she answered. "Is anything wrong?"

"Well, I don't know . . . I guess I've been a little sad lately, you know, with how slow my recovery's gone, my lack of a social life and stuff," I answered.

I can't believe I'm telling my doctor these things.

"Robert, look where you were three years ago," she said.

"Yeah, I know," I said with a half-hearted smile.

Dr. R. was right, but I was still discouraged. I knew I had to deal with my depression if my outlook on life was going to improve.

Later that evening, I received a phone call from my friend John, who had returned to Virginia after two years in Germany. We discussed everything from politics to theology, and I brought up my conversation with Dr. R.

"Rob, let me tell you something," he began, "since your relapse and bone marrow transplant, you've become a lot more serious than when I first met you."

"Really?" I asked, surprised.

"Yes," he replied. "I first noticed it when I visited you in the hospital three years ago, but I assumed that you were so sick and so focused on getting better that you couldn't think of anything else. Since my return to the States, I've noticed you're still like that."

"What do you mean exactly?" I asked.

"I'm not criticizing you or anything," he said, "but you used to have an infectious sense of humor. You were always kidding around and making people laugh."

"Hmmm . . . I guess I've changed in that area," I agreed. "It's probably because I'm more aware of how I can hurt someone's feelings if I'm teasing them. You know, I'm just more sensitive now," I answered.

"No, no. That's not what I mean," he countered. "You were never mean-spirited. I'm talking about the way you were in general. You used to have a real jocular, care-free nature about you. And I guess what I'm trying to say is that it was a real pleasant side of your personality . . . and I miss it."

I was saddened by what John had said because I knew it was true. Since my BMT, I'd lost something far more precious than my health.

What happened to my joy? My thrill of living? I'm underwhelmed by everything good that happens in my life.

I told my mom what John had said, and she commented, "Rob, you know, it really has been a while since I've heard you laugh."

So, the verdict was in. I **was** depressed. Dr. R. may have just noticed it that afternoon, but it had been brewing in me for several months. Maybe even years.

Since my BMT, I had pursued the elusive goal of getting back to normal, and I let other things fall by the wayside.

Perhaps that's why I don't have the joy that I once had. I used to be happy . . . years ago. What happened?

The answer was obvious. I was disappointed with my life, and I felt ashamed that I hadn't accomplished anything. It had been six years since I graduated from ORU, and I had yet to interview for my first real job.

Living with my parents in my late 20s so I can save money is one thing. Doing so because I have no job is different. Outside of marriage, what other rites of passage are there besides gainful employment, financial independence, and moving into my own place? I'm caught in a web of perpetual adolescence!!

I'm not sure how well my women readers can appreciate this, but there are few things that strike at a man's self-esteem more than the recognition that he hasn't spread his wings and flown. I refused to attend my 10-year high school reunion earlier that spring because I'd always envisioned myself walking into the room as Dr. Robert C. Brown, with my wife by my side. I had no intention of going there and answering questions such as, "So, Rob, what line of work are you in now?" or "Are you seeing anyone special?"

I resented my peers who had moved on with their lives. They had careers, steady girlfriends, and financial independence. Some were married.

Marriage? Yeah, right. At the rate I'm going, I can kiss off that possibility indefinitely. I haven't been on a date in two years, and I'm nowhere close to ready for a relationship. I have career aspira-

tions, not a career. That's okay if you're 19, but approaching 30? What kind of woman is going to turn her head toward me?

Younger peers who once saw me as an adult role model were now further along in life than me. Every time I heard about so-and-so who had just become engaged or accepted a job, I felt like a loser.

I resented my brother as well. He had a career, a wife, and a full head of hair. Seeing him often just reminded me that I wasn't where I wanted to be in life.

That August, I admitted that my discontent and frustration with life was based on a failure to accept things as they were, as opposed to how I wanted them to be. I knew deep down that if I continued to base my value on how well I compared with others or my happiness on the quality of my health, I'd never rediscover the joy of living. I needed a change in perspective.

Chapter XXXIX

A Change in Perspective

═══════════════════════════

That autumn, I sought individual counseling, believing it could help me come to terms with the frustration, loneliness and sense of "developmental disparity" that characterized my life. Playing the role of the victim and blaming my unhappiness on my medical condition had gotten me nowhere.

Thankfully, my therapist made it clear from the very beginning that contentment was a choice that had little to do with external factors such as a diagnosis with cancer.

"Rob," Larry said during one of our first sessions, "I've notice that you often use the word 'limited' when you describe yourself."

"Really?" I asked.

"Yes," he replied. "It seems as if you define your entire life in terms of the limitations imposed on you by your medical condition."

"Yeah, I guess I do," I admitted.

"When you view yourself as 'limited,' it keeps you from recognizing the choices you make each day that determine whether of not you enjoy life or just exist," he said. "In the midst of your preoccupation with the future — returning to full health, moving out of your parents' home, starting a career — you've forgotten the value of living in the present."

Those words were an epiphany.

He's right. I've been so fixated on what I want to happen down the line that I don't take advantage of opportunities that are available right now.

"This week, I want you to make a list of all the false beliefs that have prevented you from seeing the options you have for enjoying life now," he continued. "Bring me the list next session so we can discuss it."

That afternoon, I sat down at my Macintosh SE and pecked away at the assignment Larry had given me. When the list was completed, I was so stricken by the absurdity of it all that I couldn't contain my laughter. Among the beliefs that I listed were:

"In order for me to be a productive member of society and the church, I must be healthy."

"When I'm completely healthy, then I will do this, that, and so forth for God and others."

"Things will be great when I'm fully recovered, employed, and financially independent."

"I can't be happy until I'm off my meds and working full-time."

At the core of every one of these beliefs was the choice to be so forward-looking that I disregarded the present.

Truth is, I had far more options available to me in Autumn '96 than I did as a BMT patient three years earlier. In fact, when I put the past year in perspective, I realized that my recovery, though slow, had **not** been in a state of inertia. In the past year, I'd managed to cut my dosages of Plaquenil and Prednisone in half, reduce my daily intake of Imuran by 80 percent, and wean myself off antinausea medications altogether. Better yet, outside of a recent bout with hay fever, changes in the weather no longer put me on the brink of a respiratory infection.

Because I saw my glass as half-empty, I'd also downplayed the the fact that my career was slowly getting on track. I was half-finished with my graduate studies at Marymount University, and I was now seeing clients one night a week under the supervision of Chris, the CFC Counseling Director.

Seeing Larry forced me to assess the life I'd carved out for myself, and I didn't like what I saw. Instead of redeeming the time, I'd squandered it by feeling sorry for myself and yearning for what might be in the future. Now it was time to reverse that trend.

Chapter XL

The Great Reversal

===

Faced with the option of wallowing in self-pity or taking responsibility for my happiness, I chose the latter. Before I rang in the New Year, I made two decisions that redefined the quality of my relationships, emotional well-being, and physical health.

That December, I made a clean break from the CFC singles' ministry. The move was long in coming, but I procrastinated due to my loyalty to the group and fear of change. When I examined my motives for remaining in a ministry that now catered to an older generation, I admitted that my loyalty was based on memories. An era of my life had passed. The core group which saw me through my ordeal with cancer had left, and now it was time for me to do so as well.

Thankfully, I didn't have to look far. In response to the growing needs of my church's ever-increasing Gen-X population, a dynamic ministry by the name of "CrossCurrent" had been launched several months earlier. Although I visited the new group a few times that fall, I hesitated to get involved because, for the first time in years, I was the new kid on the block. In stark contrast to my previous group, I was also one of the oldest in the room. I wondered if I would find them immature and feared they might write me off as too old.

Joining CrossCurrent was the best decision I've made in years.

Although it took me several months to become integrated into the group, I noticed early on that they merited the investment of my time. Their passion for God and commitment to reaching the surrounding community for Christ were core values I neglected in my efforts to return to normalcy. My battle with leukemia may have deepened my understanding of God's character, but my flame needed to be rekindled. Furthermore, CrossCurrent had a vibrant small groups ministry.

In the five years since I first visited CrossCurrent, its membership has exploded from a handful of 20-something hold-overs from the Senior High youth group to 200-plus. We've outgrown two classrooms, and over the past three years, several dozen young adults from all walks of life have made decisions to live for Christ. As for myself, I've made friends, not just acquaintances. Sure I'm older than most of them, but we're all in the same stage of life. Some of us are still in school, and the rest of us are just beginning our careers. All of us are seeking a deeper relationship with God that transcends the frenzy of our postmodern culture. Every week I'm challenged to turn my focus outward instead of just dwelling on what I want God to do for me. As a result, my passion to witness about what Christ has done in my life is the highest it's been in years.

During the late summer and early fall of '96, I also became more proactive in my response to my physical limitations. Instead of ruminating over whether or not my joints would ever return to normal, I consulted an orthopedic specialist that August to assess my condition and evaluate my options for treatment. The fear of the unknown drove me crazy, and I wanted the truth from an expert.

"I haven't been using my exercise bike for almost two months because I'm afraid of causing irreparable damage to my joints," I explained.

"Well, from what I can see, your joints appear to be normal in terms of range of motion and flexibility. I could arrange for a bone scan if you'd like," he offered. "I'm not an expert on this condition. A rheumatologist might be able to give you some more definitive answers."

"I'd like the bone scan first before I see any more specialists," I said, suspecting that a rheumatologist wouldn't tell me anything different.

The following week, I went through a full-body bone scan, the results of which were the most encouraging news I'd heard since my collapsed lung reinflated in February '94.

It showed no signs of osteopeorosis, rheumatism, arthritis, or GVHD.

"So, does this mean there are no signs of permanent damage?" I questioned my orthopedist.

"That's correct," he replied.

"Does the bone scan show any problems at all?" I asked.

"There's an accumulation of blood around your ankles and knees, indicating moderate erosion of the joint lining, a condition consistent with prolonged use of corticosteroids," he replied.

"Is this problem reversible once I get off the steroids?" I asked.

"Yes," he answered.

"How about my resuming exercise on my stationary bike?" I asked. "Will that damage my knees?"

"It shouldn't be a problem If you use discretion and don't overdo it," he said.

I was ecstatic. When I told my parents, my mom said, "Rob, that's wonderful. Let this serve as a lesson to you about trusting in God."

"What do you mean?" I asked.

"Well, I've believed all along that when God said that he would heal you 'totally and completely,' he meant it. Now, has anything happened up to this time that has given you an indication that you won't get back to normal?"

"No, I guess not," I said.

"Still, though, I don't think you should overdo it on the exercise bike," she cautioned. "Take it slowly. You seem to think that in order to make up for lost time, you need to go twice as hard. You don't want another setback."

I resumed using my stationary bike a week later, and I traded in the Ace Neoprine Braces and Ben-Gay for an alternative form of treatment called "magnetic therapy." When my Aunt Pat and Uncle Joe told my father earlier that summer how much Joe's arthritis had improved since he began sleeping on a magnetic mattress cover, I was tempted to write it off as snake oil. Since my diagnosis with leukemia, I'd heard enough claims about alternative medicine to last a lifetime. I was convinced that most of them were exaggerations that couldn't be substantiated by hard science.

Although skeptical, I was determined to find a treatment that could help me until I went off Prednisone for good. I'd tried heat, ice, deep tissue massage, and physical therapy, but nothing had provided me with anything more than temporary relief. Within a few days of taping some magnets onto the insides of my knee joints and ankles, however, I was amazed at how much better they felt. For the first time in months, I could go up and down the stairs without pain and walk around shopping malls without incident!

My readers might be tempted to attribute my improvement to the so-called "placebo effect," but I'm not the only one who can attest to the effectiveness of magnetic therapy. In the past five years, experimental studies have confirmed its analgesic benefits for a broad array of joint problems. I don't know why this form of treatment works, and I don't care. It was a Godsend.

Changing my peer group and becoming proactive in response to my physical limitations was a step in the right direction. However, that was only the beginning. Finding contentment in the present was, and still is, my greatest challenge.

Chapter XLI

First Things

To date, the eighth anniversary of my BMT has passed. The medical establishment can't give me any promises, but I'm convinced the leukemia remains in the past forever. Unless the Lord returns or an unforeseen tragedy snuffs my life out, I expect to be here a very long time.

When I started writing this book in May '94, I assumed the last chapter would end with the following testimonial: *"Praise God! I'm living on my own, engaged to be married to the woman of my dreams, and I'm fully licensed as a Professional Counselor in the Commonwealth of VA. I've been medication-free for two years and my energy level is so high that I'll be competing in the Marine Corps Marathon next year."*

Like a potter committed to working with clay until fashioned to desire, God is more concerned with me as a person than whether these goals are fulfilled. In spite of God's faithfulness, I have yet to reach the point of Christian maturity where I can say with the Apostle Paul that "I have learned to be content whatever the circumstances."[1] I still yearn for the time I can wake up each morning in my own house, and I continue to dream of running barefoot

---

[1] Philippians 4:11b

without pain. For this reason, I procrastinated on finishing this book because I assumed that it would be incomplete as long as those elusive goals remained unfulfilled.

God's wisdom is higher than mine, and I know he has a purpose in my completing this book now. Perhaps he wants to use my story as an illustration of our inability to tie the loose ends of our lives together according to our own timetables. After all, that only happens in the movies. There will always be disappointments and challenges that highlight our need for God.

Contentment in my present circumstances is a decision I have to make every day. God has given me the grace to respond with a thankful heart for all he's accomplished in my life thus far, even if I'm not where I envisioned I'd be at the age of 34. Since September '96, my recovery has been remarkably steady. I've gone through six straight winters without catching the flu, and I finally became medication-free a year ago. Outside of a bout with bronchitis last summer, my health has been excellent. My joints have improved so much that I can go rock climbing, romp full-force on the stairclimber, and lift weights without pain. And this is **without** the use of magnets or joint-building supplements like *Chondroitin Glucosamine*.

I graduated from Marymount University in December '99 with an M.A. in Psychological Services, and I'm now gainfully employed as a counselor with both CFC and McLean Bible Church in McLean, VA. As I look back on my experience as a young therapist these past several years, I'm so glad I never gave up nine years ago when I questioned my suitability for my profession. Although I received my first job offer 10 years after my graduation from ORU, I couldn't have asked for a better opportunity to grow as a professional and use my gifts for the glory of God.

When I first came home from the hospital in February '94, I assumed a "total and complete" recovery would be the ultimate manifestation of God's power in my life. I'm finally on the verge of reaching that elusive goal, but it would be empty were it not for the greater work he's done in my life. When people ask me how they can know if they are following God's will, I tell them that his primary purpose for all of us is summarized in Ephesians 3:16-19:

"For this reason, I kneel before the Father, from whom his whole family in heaven and on earth derives its name. I pray that out of his glorious riches he may strengthen you with power through his Spirit in your inner being so that Christ may dwell in your hearts through faith. And I pray that you, being rooted and established in love, may have power, together with all the saints, to grasp how wide and long and high and deep is the love of Christ, and to know this love that surpasses knowledge — that you may be filled to the measure of all the fullness of God."

God wants us to be overwhelmed with the power of his love. He is so committed to this end that he allows adversity to mold us into people who encounter and reflect his love in everything we do. James urges us to respond to such tests with "pure joy" because the end result is Christian maturity.[2]

As you have gathered from reading my story, "pure joy" isn't my hall-mark response every time God puts me through the molding process. Even now I resent having to alter my plans when I have a cold or need to schedule an appointment for blood work. Nevertheless, I have no doubt that every battle I've fought since my diagnosis has deepened my faith in Christ. If you trace back through the pages of this book, you will find that God demonstrated the magnitude of his love and grace the most when I was at my weakest.

Paul experienced this as well:

"To keep me from becoming conceited because of my surpassingly great revelations, there was given me a thorn in my flesh, a messenger of Satan, to torment me. Three times I pleaded with the Lord to take it away from me. But he said to me, 'My grace is sufficient for you, for my power is made perfect in weakness.' Therefore I will boast all the more gladly about my weaknesses, so that Christ's power may rest on me. That is why, for Christ's sake, I delight in weaknesses, in insults, in hardships, in persecutions, in difficulties. For when I am weak, then I am strong."[3]

---

[2] James 1::2-4
[3] II Corinthians 12:7-10

No one knows what Paul's "thorn in the flesh" was so I won't speculate here. All that matters is that he had something in his life that he wanted God to remove. In order to teach him humility, God chose not to do so.

I can relate to Paul. If I had tapered off all my medications in Autumn '94, I would have returned to full health in a matter of months. As a result of my seven-year battle with GVHD, I can now identify with others who struggle with chronic problems that seem to lack clear solutions. I've also found that my weaknesses provide opportunities to display God's love that I never knew existed.

One such instance happened on a Monday afternoon in February '95. I had a sinus infection and the antibiotic I was taking caused so much nausea and diarrhea that Dr. R. told me to come to the clinic for a check-up.

On the way to the hospital, my dad and I hit some heavy traffic. After several instances of stopping and going, my stomach became so churned up that I vomited all over myself and the passenger seat. I felt horrible and looked a mess. I wasn't about to let Dr. R. see vomit all over me because I feared she might reserve a room for me in the hospital. After my dad let me off at the front of the building so he could park the car, I rushed to the men's room to clean myself up.

I spent the next ten minutes on the toilet, frustrated and discouraged. Just as I was about ready to give God a piece of my mind, someone else came in to use the facilities. Needing wet paper towels so I could clean my shirt and pants off, I swallowed my pride and asked, "Can whoever's out there help me with something?"

"Sure, what do you need?" he asked.

"I was on my way to see the doctor, and I vomited all over myself in the car. I hope this isn't an imposition, but could you hand me some wet paper towels over the stall so I can clean myself up?" I asked.

"No problem," he answered.

For the next five minutes, he passed towels over the wall, and I cleaned my clothes up until the smell was barely noticeable. When I came out of the stall, I shook his hand and said, "Thanks a lot. Every once in a while I get sick from all the medication I'm taking. I really appreciate your helping me in there."

"Oh, that's okay," he said.

"Are you a patient here too?" I asked.

"No, I'm just spending the night here in the waiting room because I don't have anywhere else to stay," he replied. "I came up here from Georgia for a job interview tomorrow. I haven't had a job for awhile."

"Hey, I'm sorry to hear about that. Listen, I've got to go in a couple of minutes, but I'm wondering if you would mind if I prayed for you first," I said.

"Yeah, I'd appreciate that," he answered.

With that, I joined hands with him and prayed that God would show him favor in his job interview, remind him of his love, and draw him to himself. After we finished, I gave him a few dollars for food and left.

I was a different person when I walked out of that restroom. At that moment, I was actually glad that God had allowed me to be sick at that particular time. I was given the opportunity to meet and give hope to a man who was discouraged and down on his luck. I don't know what's happened in his life since then, but I feel blessed knowing he'll probably never forget that a sick patient took the time to pray for him. I'm not bragging about myself here because if it were not for God's love working through me, I would have just thanked the man and left without a word.

When going through an experience with cancer, it's easy to be self-absorbed and forget that other people have problems. In times when I'm down, nothing helps me regain perspective better than reaching out to someone who is in worse pain. Whether it's encouraging a prospective BMT patient or using my testimony as a vehicle for sharing my faith, I'm humbled every time God uses me in spite of my hardheadedness. Three years ago, I even had the opportunity to lead a 20-year-old leukemia patient to Christ. Christian (aptly named, I might add) went home to be with the Lord on Christmas Eve '98. His mom later told me that at the time of his death, he was a completely different person. The love of God had impacted his life for all eternity.

No one knows just how deep his faith is until it's put to the test. I'm thankful that since that fateful ER experience in June '92, I've never had to work up the strength to trust God. The key to trusting

God is knowing he'll supply the grace to persevere in the face of chaos.

People often tell me and my family that we're an inspiration and a great example of faith. That may be so, but none of us can take the credit. Throughout my battle with leukemia, God never let us go through anything without supplying the power to trust him. Every time it seemed things could get no worse, he reminded us that he was the Master Potter. All we had to do was entrust ourselves to his care and feed on the truth of his Word.

My battle with leukemia was the defining moment of my life. If you had asked me what I valued in life 10 years ago, I would have rambled on and on about the goals I set for myself: earning my Doctorate, finding a wife, buying my first home, and starting a family. These things are still important to me, but my experience with cancer has shown me that the ordinary, everyday things in life are often the most meaningful.

This revelation, if you want to call it that, came to me one spring day six years ago. Everything was in full glory — the dogwoods, the azaleas, and the sunshine casting shadows across the lush foothills of Virginia. There couldn't have been a better day for a postcard snapshot. On my drive home from church that afternoon, I caught a whiff of freshly mowed grass, a fragrance I hadn't smelled for a long time. I'd forgotten how much I missed that smell while I was in the hospital, and I thanked God for allowing me to experience it again.

The smell of rain in April, the way my grandmother lights up like a Christmas tree whenever she sees me, the pleasure of watching Graycee chase a squirrel across the yard . . . these make life special. Especially if you have people with whom you can share them.

It wouldn't have been possible without God, but the fact I'm alive today is also a testament to my family. My relationship with my parents is the best it's ever been. Living with them as an adult has helped me grow to appreciate their love, counsel, and friendship. The most remarkable turn-around here has been my relationship with my dad. His honesty, integrity, humility, and humor continue to keep me grounded. When I reflect back on how David, Brenda, and my extended family responded to my diagnosis, I become all the more convinced that a loving family is a wonderful heritage.

If there is anything that I leave with my readers, I hope it's an appreciation of God's love, the blessing of family and friends, the value of the ordinary, and the wisdom of the Potter. I consider these "first things" because in the final analysis, they're the only things that matter.

The End

Potter's Hand

Beautiful Lord, Wonderful Savior
I Know For Sure All Of My Days
Are Held In Your Hand
Crafted Into Your Perfect Plan

You Gently Call Me Into Your Presence
Guiding Me By Your Holy Spirit
Teach me, Dear Lord, To Live All Of My Life
Through Your Eyes

I'm Captured By Your Holy Calling
Set Me Apart
I know You're Drawing Me To Yourself
Lead Me Lord, I Pray

Take Me, Mold Me
Use Me, Fill Me
I Give My Life To The Potter's Hand

Call Me, Guide Me
Lead Me, Walk Beside Me
I Give My Life To The Potter's Hand

Darlene Zschech
Copyright © 1998 Hillsongs Austrailia

Appendix

================================

The following Scripture passages have influenced me the most since my diagnosis. Most of them were given to me by friends or family members at various times during my leukemia experience, and they turned me heavenward when things couldn't get much worse. Their message is timeless. If you were to read just one chapter in my book, I hope it would be this.

Psalm 46:1-2

> "God is our refuge and strength, an ever present help in trouble. Therefore we will not fear, though the earth give way and the mountains fall into the heart of the sea, though its waters roar and foam and the mountains quake with their surging."

Isaiah 26:3

> "You will keep in perfect peace him whose mind is steadfast, because he trusts in you."

Isaiah 43:2

> "When you pass through the waters, I will be with you;

and when you pass through the rivers, they will not sweep over you. When you walk through the fire, you will not be burned; the flames will not set you ablaze."

Romans 8:28

"And we know that in all things God works for the good of those who love him, who have been called according to his purpose."

II Corinthians 1:3-4

"Praise be to the God and Father of our Lord Jesus Christ, the Father of compassion and the God of all comfort, who comforts us in all our troubles, so that we can comfort those in any trouble with the comfort we ourselves have received from God."

II Corinthians 1:8-10

"We do not want you to be uninformed, brothers, about the hardships we suffered in the province of Asia. We were under great pressure, far beyond our ability to endure, so that we despaired even of life. Indeed in our hearts we felt the sentence of death. But this happened that we might not rely on ourselves but on God, who raises the dead. He has delivered us from such a deadly peril, and he will deliver us. On him we have set our hope that he will continue to deliver us."

II Timothy 1:7

"For God did not give us a spirit of timidity, but a spirit of power, of love and of self-discipline."

Philippians 4:6-7

"Do not be anxious about anything, but in everything, by

prayer and petition, with thanksgiving, present your requests to God. And the peace of God, which transcends all understanding, will guard your hearts and your minds in Christ Jesus."

Philippians 4:13

"I can do everything through him who gives me strength."

Philippians 4:20

"And my God will meet all your needs according to his glorious riches in Christ Jesus."

Romans 12:12

"Be joyful in hope, patient in affliction, faithful in prayer."

James 5:13-18

"Is anyone of you in trouble? He should pray. Is anyone happy? Let him sing songs of praise. Is anyone of you sick? He should call the elders of the church to pray over him and anoint him with oil in the name of the Lord. And the prayer offered in faith will make the sick person well; the Lord will raise him up. If he has sinned, he will be forgiven. Therefore confess your sins to each other so that you may be healed. The prayer of a righteous man is powerful and effective. Elijah was a man just like us. He prayed earnestly that it would not rain, and it did not rain on the land for three and a half years. Again he prayed, and the heavens gave rain, and the earth produced its crops."

Mark 11:22-23

"'Have faith in God,' Jesus answered. 'I tell you the truth, if anyone says to this mountain, "Be removed and be cast into the sea," and does not doubt in his heart, but believes that what he says will happen, it will be done for him.'"

John 14:12-14

"'I tell you the truth, anyone who has faith in me will do what I have been doing. He will do even greater things than these, because I am going to the Father. And I will do whatever you ask in my name, so that the Son may bring glory to the Father. You may ask me for anything in my name, and I will do it.'"

John 16:23-24

"'In that day you will no longer ask me anything. I tell you the truth, my father will give you whatever you ask for in my name. Until now you have not asked for anything in my name. Ask and you will receive, and your joy will be complete.'"

Luke 11:9-10

"'So I say to you, ask and it will be given to you; seek and you will find; knock and the door will be opened to you. For everyone who asks receives; he who seeks finds; and to him who knocks, the door will be opened.'"

Hebrews 11:1-6

"Now faith is being sure of what we hope for and certain of what we do not see. This is what the ancients were commended for. By faith we understand that the universe was formed at God's command, so that what is seen was not made out of what was visible. By faith Abel offered God a better sacrifice than Cain did. By faith he was commended as a righteous man, when God spoke well of his offerings. And by faith he still speaks, even though he is dead. By faith Enoch was taken from this life, so that he did not experience death; he could not be found, because God had taken him away. For before he was taken, he was commended as one who pleased God. And without faith it is impossible to please God, because anyone who comes to him must believe that he exists and that he rewards those who earnestly seek him."

Matthew 9:20

"Just then a woman who had been subject to bleeding for twelve years came up behind him and touched the edge of his cloak. She said to herself, 'If I only touch his cloak, I will be healed.'

"Jesus turned and saw her. 'Take heart daughter,' he said, 'your faith has healed you.' And the woman was healed from that very moment."

Matthew 10:27-30

"As Jesus went on from there, two blind men followed him, calling out, 'Have mercy on us, Son of David!'

"When he had gone indoors, the blind men came to him, and he asked them, 'Do you believe that I am able to do this?'

"'Yes, Lord,' they replied.

"Then he touched their eyes and said, 'According to your faith will it be done to you,' and their sight was restored."

Matthew 8:2-3

"A man with leprosy came and knelt before him and said, 'Lord, if you are willing, you can make me clean.' Jesus reached out and touched the man. 'I am willing,' he said. 'Be clean!' Immediately he was cured of his leprosy."

I John 5:14-15

"This is the assurance we have in approaching God; that if we ask anything according to his will, he hears us. And if we know that he hears us — whatever we ask — we know that we have what we asked of him."

Romans 12:1-2

"Therefore, I urge you, brothers, in view of God's mercy, to offer your bodies as living sacrifices, holy and pleasing to God — which is your spiritual worship. Do not conform any longer to the pattern of this world, but be transformed by the renewing of your mind. Then you will be able to test and approve what God's will is — his good, pleasing and perfect will."

Exodus 15:26

"He said, 'If you listen carefully to the voice of the LORD your God and do what is right in his eyes, if you pay attention to his commands and keep all his decrees, I will not bring on you any of the diseases I brought on the Egyptians, for I am the LORD who heals you.'"

Exodus 23:25

"'Worship the LORD your God, and his blessing will be on your food and water. I will take away sickness from among you, and none will miscarry or be barren in your land. I will give you a full life span.'"

Proverbs 4:20-23

"My son, pay attention to what I say; listen closely to my words. Do not let them out of your sight, keep them within your heart; for they are life to those who find them and health to a man's whole body."

Proverbs 9:10-11

"'The fear of the LORD is the beginning of wisdom, and knowledge of the Holy One is understanding. For through me your days will be many, and years will be added to your life.'"

Proverbs 22:4

"Humility and the fear of the LORD bring wealth, honor and life."

Psalm 107:20-21

"He sent his word and healed them; he rescued them from the grave. Let them give thanks to the LORD for his unfailing love and his wonderful deeds for men."

Jeremiah 17:14

"'Heal me, O LORD, and I will be healed; save me and I will be saved, for you are the One I praise.'"

Hebrews 4:12

"The word of God is living and active. Sharper than any double-edged sword, it penetrates even to dividing soul and spirit, joints and marrow; it judges the thoughts and attitudes of the heart."

II Corinthians 10:4-5

"The weapons we fight with are not the weapons of the world. On the contrary, they have divine power to demolish strongholds. We demolish arguments and every pretension that sets itself up against the knowledge of God, and we take captive every thought to make it obedient to Christ."

Numbers 23:19

"'God is not a man that he should lie, nor a son of man, that he should change his mind. Does he speak and then not act? Does he promise and not fulfill?'"

Joshua 21:45

"Not one of the LORD's good promises to the house of Israel failed: every one was fulfilled."

I Samuel 12:16

"'Now then, stand still and see this great thing the LORD is about to do before your eyes!'"

Psalm 103:1-5

"Praise the LORD, O my soul; all my inmost being, praise his holy name.

"Praise the LORD, O my soul, and forget not all his benefits.

"He forgives all my sins and heals all my diseases; he redeems my life from the pit and crowns me with love and compassion.

"He satisfies my desires with good things so that my youth is renewed like the eagle's."

Jeremiah 29:11-13

"'For I know the plans I have for you,' declares the LORD, 'plans to prosper you and not to harm you, plans to give you hope and a future. Then you will call upon me and come and pray to me, and I will listen to you. You will seek me and find me when you seek me with all your heart.'"

Jeremiah 32:27

"'I am the LORD, the God of all mankind. Is anything too hard for me?'"

II Corinthians 1:20

"For no matter how many promises God has made, they are 'Yes' in Christ. And so through him the 'Amen' is spoken by us to the glory of God."

Isaiah 53:4-5

"Surely he took up our infirmities and carried our sorrows, yet we considered him stricken by God, smitten by him and afflicted.[1]

"But he was pierced for our transgressions, he was crushed for our iniquities; the punishment that brought us peace was upon him, and by his wounds we are healed."

Matthew 8:14-17

"When Jesus came into Peter's house, he saw Peter's mother-in-law lying in bed with a fever. He touched her hand and the fever left her, and she got up and began to wait on him. When evening came, many who were demon-possessed were brought to him, and he drove out spirits with a word and healed all the sick. This was to fulfill what was spoken through the prophet Isaiah: 'He took up our infirmities and carried our diseases.'"

Matthew 9:35

"Jesus went through all the towns and villages, teaching

---

[1] The Hebrew word for "Sorrows" in this verse is more properly translated as "Diseases." See Matthew 8:17.

in the synagogues, preaching the good news of the king-dom and healing every disease and sickness."

John 10:10

"'The thief come only to steal and kill and destroy: I have come that they may have life, and have it to the full.'"

Hebrews 13:8

"Jesus Christ is the same yesterday and today and forever."

Bibliography

Better Homes and Gardens Family Medical Guide. Ed. Donald G. Cooley. New York: Better Homes and Gardens Books, 1976.

Crabb, Larry Jr. *Finding God*. Grand Rapids, MI: Zondervan Publishing House, 1993.

Zschech, Darlene. "Potter's Hand." *Touching Heaven Changing Earth*. Hillsongs Austrailia, 1998.

Halvorson-Boyd, Glenna, and Hunter, Lisa K. "Cancer Changes Our Lives — And Our Relationships." *Coping* May/June 1997: 68-70.

Leukemia Society of America. *Bone Marrow Transplantation (BMT)*. New York: Program Services Department of Leukemia Society of America, 1992.

Marshall, Catherine. *Adventures in Prayer*. Grand Rapids, MI: Chosen books, 1975.

National Cancer Institute. *Research Report: Bone Marrow Transplant*. 1991 ed. Washington, D.C.: U.S. Department of Human Services, 1991.

National Cancer Institute. *Research Report: Leukemia*. 1987 ed. Washington, D.C.: U.S. Department of Human Services, 1987.

"Post-transplant Infections." *BMT Newsletter* September 1994: 1-6.

The Signet Mosby Medical Encyclopedia. Ed. Walter D.Glanze, Kenneth N. Anderson, and Lois E. Anderson. Rev. ed. New York: Penguin Books USA Inc., 1996.

Printed in the United States
913400003B